When Core Values Are Strategic

When Core Values Are Strategic

How the Basic Values of Procter & Gamble Transformed Leadership at Fortune 500 Companies

Rick Tocquigny
with Andy Butcher

Vice President, Publisher: Tim Moore
Associate Publisher and Director of Marketing: Amy Neidlinger
Executive Editor/Acquisitions Editor: Tim Moore and Mike Vaccaro
Editorial Assistant: Pamela Boland
Development Editor: Russ Hall
Operations Specialist: Jodi Kemper
Senior Marketing Manager: Julie Phifer
Assistant Marketing Manager: Megan Graue
Cover Designer: Chuti Prasertsith
Managing Editor: Kristy Hart
Project Editors: Samantha Sinkhorn and Jovana Shirley
Copy Editor: Karen Gill
Proofreader: Sarah Kearns
Compositor: Nonie Ratcliff
Manufacturing Buyer: Dan Uhrig

© 2012 by P&G Alumni Network, Inc.
Publishing as FT Press
Upper Saddle River, New Jersey 07458

FT Press offers excellent discounts on this book when ordered in quantity for bulk purchases or special sales. For more information, please contact U.S. Corporate and Government Sales, 1-800-382-3419, corpsales@pearsontechgroup.com. For sales outside the U.S., please contact International Sales at international@pearson.com.

Company and product names mentioned herein are the trademarks or registered trademarks of their respective owners.

Procter & Gamble and P&G are trade names of The Procter & Gamble Company and are used pursuant to an agreement with The Procter & Gamble Company. P&G Alumni Network is an independent organization apart from The Procter & Gamble Company.

Printed in the United States of America
Second Printing February 2012

ISBN-10: 0-13-290533-7
ISBN-13: 978-0-13-290533-6

Pearson Education LTD.
Pearson Education Australia PTY, Limited.
Pearson Education Singapore, Pte. Ltd.
Pearson Education Asia, Ltd.
Pearson Education Canada, Ltd.
Pearson Educación de Mexico, S.A. de C.V.
Pearson Education—Japan
Pearson Education Malaysia, Pte. Ltd.

Library of Congress Cataloging-in-Publication Data:

Tocquigny, Rick, 1955-
  When core values are strategic : how the basic values of Procter & Gamble transformed leadership at Fortune 500 companies / Rick Tocquigny.
    p. cm.
  ISBN 978-0-13-290533-6 (hbk. : alk. paper)
1. Procter & Gamble Company--Management. 2. Executives--Case studies. 3. Leadership. 4. Values. 5. Customer relations. 6. Organizational effectiveness. I. Title.
  HD9999.S74P768 2012
  658.4'012--dc23
                          2011038704

Contents

Foreword

I served at Procter & Gamble (P&G) from 1977 to 2010—more than half my life. One of the great benefits of my tenure was being immersed in, and surrounded by, the core values and purpose of a nearly 174-year-old company. P&G's purpose focuses *externally* and *strategically* on consumers' needs and wants...and on brands, products, and innovation to improve consumers' lives. The values are important because they guide our behavior with *all* stakeholders...and each other.

R.R. Deupree, who led the company through the 1930s' depression and through World War II, used to say that if you leave P&G's money, its buildings, and its brands but take away its people, the business will be in real jeopardy. But if you take away the money, the buildings, and the brands, but *leave the people*, it will rebuild a comparable new business in as little as a decade. Mr. Deupree knew what he was talking about, because that's what P&G people—led by purpose and guided by values—have essentially done throughout their history. As a rule, each generation of P&G people has, in fact, built the equivalent of a new business the size of the previous, existing business in about a decade.

Our sales today are roughly double what they were 10 years ago, and those sales are roughly double those of the decade prior. P&G business portfolios have outperformed the market during up and down cycles alike, and we're one of only 10 companies that have remained on Fortune's top 50 American-based companies since the ranking began in 1955.

P&G's core purpose and values have served as the foundation for our success, generation after generation. They have allowed us to adapt quickly and strategically, which, in turn, has promoted consistent and sustainable growth. This is the fabric of our company. It is our culture. And it is, in part, why P&G is uniquely special—for its core values and for the number of world-class leaders that have come through this culture, touching and improving the lives of consumers around the world and enhancing the welfare of employees and share owners.

Through the quite varied individual voices, with stories that span over five decades, you will hear how the purpose and values of P&G became a strategic point of difference for the company and other organizations these leaders went on to manage. The stories reveal the DNA of a "P&Ger"—that innate, values-driven commitment to make consumers' lives a little bit better...every day.

You will read the intriguing story of Bryce Harlow, P&G's legendary head of Government Relations, and how he influenced Presidents Eisenhower, Kennedy, Johnson, Nixon, Ford, Reagan, and Carter. You will learn about P&G's initiatives, such as "Live, Learn, and Thrive," that represent P&G's core values at work. You will hear from colleagues and friends like Charlotte Otto, who, during the 2000s, helped me restore the confidence of P&G people by reinvigorating our values and strategically leveraging P&G's purpose.

There are many inspiring stories that illustrate former Chairman and CEO Ed Artz's observation...how amazing it was to think of all the different people who have worked for P&G, all so different, yet who have perpetuated a common standard of excellence across businesses of all kinds, across continents, across cultures, across decades. With P&G as the thread, you explore how core values can promote clarity of thought, in both professional and personal settings. It is a relevant, timely, and insightful message for students, small business owners, community leaders, corporations, and their leadership.

The stories in this book celebrate the gift we were all given—core values that *really work*. And they show how robust focus on core values adds great enterprise value *and* value to your personal life. Core values at work can bring out more engagement, more fulfillment, better work-life balance, and long-term business and financial success for your organizations, yourself, and the communities in which you live and work. May you be inspired to embrace your own core values and have the courage to live by them. They will serve you well over a long and successful journey.

—A.G. Lafley

Acknowledgments

To have released a book on core values at this point in time seems, on reflection, to have been fortuitous. Companies across the world are searching for their own values and cherishing leadership that steps up with a belief system that employees and shareholders can trust and build upon.

To Rick Tocquigny and Andy Butcher, your thought construction, interviewing, and writing of this book will ultimately help our Alumni Network achieve its mission to give back to the communities in which we live and work.

To the more than thirty contributors, we are grateful for your special voice and stories that made this book truly unique. Your chapters represent the thousands of dedicated employees who make core values a part of their daily lives.

Tim Moore, who is Vice President and Publisher of FT Press, provided access to the resources of Pearson, the world's largest publisher. Michael Vaccaro, Director of Pearson's Business Development, provided an energetic, can-do attitude behind this project. Both supported *When Core Values Are Strategic* along every step of the way.

Russ Hall, our Development Editor, brought our content into an enjoyable book that will inspire the next generation of leaders. His exact messaging brought clarity and flow to our stories.

Our thanks also extend to Project Editors, Samantha Sinkhorn and Jovana Shirley, and to Chuti Prasertsith, who designed the cover for the book.

We are also grateful for the administrative team at www.artbeatofamerica.com and the Life Lessons Radio network led by Carla Tocquigny, for their countless hours devoted to interviewing and logging stories. Carla is Rick's best friend, partner, and wife, and she serves to continually remind him that the best experiences in life are those that truly transform you. We also extend our special thanks to Marcie Butcher, for keeping all the pieces together, Heidi Ippolito for her hard work in transcribing all the interviews, and Jonathan Clements of Wheelhouse Lit for his insightful guidance.

This book was not written in a few months but over the lifetime of the individuals featured in *When Core Values Are Strategic*. We have been fortunate to have journeyed with such outstanding people and are forever indebted to the hundreds of thousands of P&G alumni who lived out these core values. We hope that the representative voices will inspire companies, communities, organizations, and individuals to rise to new levels of leadership with core values as their cornerstone.

—The P&G Alumni Network

About the Authors

Rick Tocquigny is a nationally known author, radio/podcast talk show host, and CEO of Artbeat of America, publisher of the *Life Lessons* book series, *The Transformed Traveler*, and Gracefully Yours greeting cards. He serves as the Chair of the P&G Alumni Network Publishing and Speakers Bureau. His Life Lessons network has been instrumental in changing the pattern of communication within companies and communities. Rick and his wife Carla live in Lafayette, Colorado. Their two daughters, Heather and Jennifer, are both in the entertainment industry and residing in Southern California. Learn more at www.artbeatofamerica.com or email lifelessonsradio@gmail.com.

Andy Butcher is an award-winning journalist and author. A former newspaper reporter and Media Director for an international non-profit, he currently edits a national trade publication.

Preface

Procter & Gamble (P&G) has long been recognized as one of the leading companies in the world. Its record of success in building brands and developing talent is unmatched. Over the years, many people who began at P&G have gone on to outstanding careers in other endeavors, taking with them the values, training, skills, and experiences gained at the company to run some of the largest organizations in the world.

The P&G Alumni Network includes more than 18,000 of these talented individuals around the world. The network is dedicated to sharing the talents and experiences of these professionals to benefit companies, nonprofits, governments, and individuals everywhere. This book is just one example of projects developed to share their perspectives. Moreover, every dollar of the P&G Alumni Network's share of book proceeds will go to our philanthropic foundation serving people around the world.

We hope you will enjoy the insights found in this book and that they will be valuable to you.

—Edward C. Tazzia
Chairman of the Board
P&G Alumni Network

Part I
Sustaining Industry Leadership

1

Core Values Can Be Strategic

Open a newspaper, turn on the television news, or flip through any number of Internet sites, and it won't take you long to find the stories of individuals, families, communities, and whole companies that have lost their way in the frantic chaos of existing and doing business these days. From the shifty ethics of giant energy companies to the shaky doings of a few media companies, some people just don't seem to be anchored in values. Worse, companies that think they should make it often don't. What went wrong? More than likely, they have gotten turned around on their path toward success because the principles for the way they did business weren't driven by their core values.

What are core values? They are the tenets by which a company, community, or family operates. A value might be focusing on the benefit to consumer—in the quality, function, and safety of products. It might be having a clear vision, valuing teamwork, or seeking to change lives for the better. A core value could certainly be striving to do the right thing.

Values differ from company to company, but at Procter & Gamble (P&G), core values help create organizational form in their own unique context. Former CEO Ed Harness once said, "Though our greatest asset is our people, it is the consistency of principle and policy that gives us direction." With that in mind, P&G makes core values strategic by finding and hiring outstanding men and women of the highest character, treating each employee as an individual who has his or her own unique talents and life goals, and providing for each employee a working environment that encourages, recognizes, and rewards individual and team achievements. As an employee, your ideas are welcomed...from day one. New employees learn about the heritage and history of their company. They hear about honesty, fairness, tradition, and integrity. Not only do they see character in action, but they begin to live out responsibility, dedicating themselves to constant improvement, being uncompromising, planning for long-term growth, making the hard decisions, and practicing disciplined and consistent thinking while having a vision to change lives.

These values become strategic when a company considers every decision based on what matters most: how to hire and keep top-quality people, how to react when a product threatens to harm consumers, and how to train and nurture employees for top performance. Those who continue to accomplish great things once they leave the company reflect on P&G's reputation as one of the finest training grounds in corporate America and the world, which doesn't hurt P&G's future recruitment.

As you read on, you will explore the stories of individuals who experienced an uncommon sculpturing of their leadership skills and strategies through core values that the 175-year-old Procter & Gamble Company instilled within them. Their stories represent the experiences of thousands of employees who were part of a company that is genuinely concerned not only with results, but with how results are achieved. Today, these leaders are changing lives by applying core values they learned within Fortune 500 companies and leading nonprofit organizations. The greater message—one that can have a huge impact on your own life or on the success of your family, community, or company—will come in recognizing how unchanging core values can become a strategic force in creating and perpetuating your long-term success.

2

Brad Moore

Brad Moore says that storytelling that changes lives is all about character—in more ways than one. The President of Hallmark Hall of Fame Productions says the importance is not just in the character of the protagonists of a drama, but of the character of those behind the productions, the values they espouse and want to communicate. As the leader for almost 30 years of the TV movie organization that has won 80 Emmys in its 60-year history, Moore places high value on the responsibility of aiming to touch people's emotions. His years with Procter & Gamble (P&G) had a significant part in shaping that conviction.

"People ask me about the differences between Procter & Gamble and Hallmark Cards," he says, "and I say that their similarities are far more important than their differences. Both companies I've had the privilege to work for have exemplary character and high ethical standards. Both always try to do what's right for people, what's right for employees, what's right for consumers, and what's right for customers. Do they have different personalities? Absolutely. But their exemplary character is the same."

Moore arrived at P&G almost by accident of wardrobe. One day in grad school, he was dressed in a suit, for reasons he doesn't now recall. A classmate told him that a late cancellation had just left an opening with visiting P&G recruiters. Moore decided that since he was dressed for the part, a practice interview wouldn't hurt. He signed up for the open slot on the schedule. "I think my approach that day caught the recruiter a little off balance because everybody who interviewed with Procter in those days was really on their best behavior and kind of begging. I was unprepared, so my approach didn't try to impress them with research and knowledge about the company, thereby demonstrating my interest in working there. Instead, I tried to turn the interview around by asking, 'Why do you, personally, like working at Procter & Gamble? Is it satisfying? Why do you think I should want to work there?' I didn't ask it in an arrogant way, but I don't think they got those kinds of questions very often. I asked them what they admired most about the company and why. As it turned out, I learned a lot that day and went on to ask the same thing in interviews with other companies. They didn't answer the questions as unflinchingly or as well as the P&G interviewer and subsequent P&Gers did."

Ultimately, though, it wasn't just their answers that persuaded Moore to join P&G in the face of other offers. "I decided that of all the people I met from many companies during the interview process, the people at P&G were the ones I liked most, and also were the ones who impressed me most. That's how I made my decision to work there. My thinking was that when you join an organization, you become part of a particular culture or subculture, especially if you're planning to be there long term. That culture will tend to shape you, because you're likely to become more like the people you're around. I thought, 'These are people I'd like to be like.'"

His decision-making about people is still consistent with that experience. "It's pretty much instinctive. It always boils down to two or three things for me: Do you trust this person? In other words, are they going to always tell the truth and try to do what's right? Next, do they work really hard? Because I do. And, are they smart? My conclusion was that P&G had been hiring people using those criteria for a long time, though maybe not described exactly that way."

During his time with P&G, Moore worked in both the "food" and "cleaning products" divisions, serving as Brand Manager and Associate Advertising Manager. His first eight years were with the coffee division, where he learned firsthand about the emotional connection between consumers and brands. "I learned that in a food category—something you ingest, actually take inside yourself—there can be a strong emotional connection with a brand, especially with coffee," he says. "It's a kind of social expression product. You drink coffee to perk up. You drink coffee to calm down. And you drink coffee with others, to socialize. It turns out some of the emotional aspects of coffee weren't all that different for me than what I found later in the greeting card business."

Another lesson was the importance of keeping things positive. The "coffee wars" occurred when Folgers, a 100+ year-old brand, which P&G had acquired in the 1960s, pushed ahead to finally complete national expansion. In doing so, it battled for national marketplace leadership with Maxwell House, another venerable brand. Competing advertisements from both sides began focusing on how bad coffee could be if it wasn't made correctly (that is, with the right brand) and how the brand being advertised was the only dependable, tasty choice.

"You had these two huge advertisers constantly talking about all the problems that coffee could have. Millions of dollars were spent in talking about the negatives of the coffee category, and the total coffee category was declining and declining, being replaced by consumers with soft drinks and other beverages with fewer potential 'problems,'" Moore recalls. "Finally, and I can happily say I was part of the beginning of this, there was a big turnaround in the approach of advertising coffee. Folgers moved to a new campaign: 'The best part of waking up is Folgers in your cup.' It was entirely positive. It wasn't negative about the other guy, just positive about Folgers. That's a good lesson: that it's better to promote the positives of your own product rather than to try pointing out the negatives of another. When everybody talked about potential negatives, the whole category went downhill. I wish politicians would learn that."

Transferring later to "packaged soaps and detergents," Moore became part of another shift within P&G. He was assigned to oversee four dishwashing liquids that had until that point been managed separately all the way up through the Associate Advertising Manager level—the thinking being that kept them more competitive, even with other P&G brands. Moore's task was to keep that internal competitive edge while also coordinating the brands to stave off competition from a new rival brand coming in from the UK, Sunlight. "That was one of the most interesting assignments I had," Moore says. "Subsequently, once I had left the company, there was a lot of press about 'category management' being introduced at P&G. I was privileged to be on the forefront of that. Brands were always coordinated, but not previously at the management level that I got to experience. Earlier on, as a brand manager, you focused on one brand and guided all aspects of that brand in competing with both internal and external brands. That's part of the superb training and experience you get in brand management at P&G: Early on in your career, you get to be a generalist. You get to work with the packaging and the performance of the product; the advertising and promotion; the distribution and pricing; the research and business analysis; everything about the brand. That's why P&G brand managers tend to have a pretty mature look at business early on in their careers. Add to that the way they're recruited and trained, it's no wonder they're also so competitive."

The son and grandson of ministers, Moore grew up in a storytelling household, but he saw the craft in different form while at P&G. From envisioning coffee ads that didn't leave a bitter taste in the television viewer's mouth, Moore further developed his understanding of the importance of emphasizing a product's benefits in the household products world. "Let's say a product really gets dirt out of your clothes or grease off your dishes in a particular way. The functional benefit, therefore, is that your clothes or dishes get clean. But the 'end' benefit is that you feel good about doing that for yourself or for others in your family." He admired the Downy fabric softener advertising (and which he readily admits he never worked on), where the camera featured the bottle falling in slow motion into a pile of towels. Soft! "But the true 'end' benefit was captured when a little girl ran up and jumped on her granddad's lap, and he wrapped her in his sweater. What a powerful demonstration of the real benefit being the 'end' benefit, the human benefit. The best advertising comes back to communicating the most compelling 'end' benefit of a product."

"It's not always obvious what that is," Moore says. "That kind of emotion is a stretch for some brands. But tapping into emotion doesn't just mean dealing with family or relationships or sentiment. For example, pride in personal effort and accomplishment can also be very emotional. Just look at Nike and Gatorade and similar products. They have true functional benefits, but also strong emotional values. Or the pride of using Apple products: Great functional benefits? Yes. But the meticulous external design, packaging, and other aspects of marketing make Apple products very 'cool' to its enthusiastic fans. That's as important to Apple's brand appeal as the purely functional aspects of its products. If you can communicate with people in a way that connects them with a brand both functional and emotionally… that's the most powerful advertising and marketing."

Moore sees a common core between his moviemaking responsibilities and his P&G past. "At Hallmark, we really believe in the power of a brand, and that's obviously a real similarity with Procter & Gamble, a company that epitomizes a strong belief in the loyalty, esteem, and trust a consumer can have for a brand. In addition to ethical principles to guide it, both companies have that in common. What the Hallmark brand stands for is something that drew me—and many of my current colleagues—to Hallmark. It's something I also had an instinct for when I joined P&G. I wouldn't have wanted to work for a company that didn't have a great reputation overall plus high consumer esteem for its brands."

Although principles do not change, styles do, and that has been true in Hallmark's films through the years. "With the increased competition on television today, the pace has to be faster," Moore says. "When I started making movies for Hallmark, there were essentially three networks. Now we're competing with another 200 or 300 choices. We have to engage the viewer more quickly and keep the story moving more quickly. Also, you really need to have the enjoyment factor higher. If viewers are going to sit down and spend the evening with you, they want enjoyment. But our principles guide us to do more than that. We strive not only to entertain but also to inspire and ensure that our movies embody what our chairman calls 'constructive intent.' We never preach, but our movies always try to convey good values, authenticity, and to somehow enrich the lives of our viewers."

One more similarity Moore sees between Hallmark and his former employer is a strong commitment to "manage the business for the long term." He says that always outweighs short-term interest in both organizations, which is perhaps more remarkable for P&G than for Hallmark, a private, family-owned company. "Our owners don't have to worry nearly as much about quarterly earnings. Procter & Gamble does, and still I remember distinctly how the company was managed for the long term. Decisions were made on what was right for the long term, not what was expedient at the time."

"I've been really fortunate to be in two companies where I've never had to question the values of the people that are in positions of leadership—where principles are what matter, not expedience, where they invest in employees by training and evaluating and mentoring. Then in the marketplace they keep focused on the consumer. That's who we're here to serve. Both P&G and Hallmark have the intent and ability to deliver great value to consumers while never sacrificing core values of the company."

3

Jane Hoover

If values and principles are challenged by the politics of business and tested by the business of politics, they are positively endangered when the worlds of business and politics intersect. Although special interest lobbying has fallen into low regard in the era of the Jack Abramoff scandal, it has an honorable history seeded by Procter & Gamble (P&G) and witnessed close up by Jane Fawcett Hoover.

Retiring from the company in 2005 as Vice President of Government Relations in Washington D.C., her near-30 years representing P&G in the Capitol, built on the foundations laid by the man credited with embodying the lobbyist's virtues more than any other single person. Bryce Harlow, a near-legendary figure who served four presidents and gave his name to the foundation that continues to promote personal integrity and public service as advocacy's plumb line, hired Hoover for his small team in 1977. In the 18 months she worked for him before his retirement, Hoover found Harlow to be "a man of many virtues. He was intellectually honest. He was straightforward. He was known for his integrity. His word was his bond. He was values-driven. He didn't compromise his principles." Having joined P&G in 1961, Harlow made his mark for his role in successfully opposing a consumer protection agency proposal by the Johnson administration that would have been overly burdensome on business and bureaucratically costly. His efforts in forming a coalition of trade groups to campaign against the plan, which was defeated, sealed his reputation as "the consummate corporate representative," Hoover recalls. "Bryce used to say a good representative of good corporations contributes a great deal to good government," Hoover adds. "This was the mantra of the office and the government relations work ever since."

In the time she saw Harlow in action, Hoover learned "the value of transparency, of being open, being straightforward, direct. I would be sitting in his office and the phone would ring and it would be Lyndon Johnson. Bryce would be talking to him about many of the political issues, and the other phone would ring and he would have to put Johnson on hold, because the current President was calling...it was truly amazing." One of the reasons that so many leaders reached out to Harlow was that "he was totally trusted," she says. "That was one of his strengths in dealing with individuals of both parties. He was often asked if he would ever write a book about his experiences. He promised that he never would because he believed that his communications with individuals should be private, built on trust, and that stories should never be shared outside of school." Although she got to hear Harlow in conversation with former and current political leaders across the spectrum, "I never heard him disparage a political party, or a person. He treated everyone with respect, always valuing sound public policy and honest public service."

"In a Harlow quote I often repeat," Hoover said, "'If informed, responsible citizens will devote an increasing share of their organizational skills and ability to influence public affairs, then America's liberty and America's future will be secure.'"

From Harlow, Hoover learned the importance of "being incredibly thorough and looking at both sides of an issue"—a lesson she put into practice when she rose to leadership in the company's government affairs office. "One of the reasons we were successful in the federal arena is that we would educate as well as advocate with a member of Congress. I would always talk with that Congressional member about our position and our opponent's point of view. I would tell them who they could talk with or where they could go to learn the other side—but I always made sure that our arguments were far stronger and better. That practice epitomized Bryce. It was all about being thorough and passionate."

In the years following Harlow's departure, "one of the individuals that enhanced the effectiveness of our office was Marvin Womack," Hoover says. Having coming up through the company as a Plant Manager and Product Supply Vice President, he "understood the needs of business units and brought about new thinking of how Washington offices should be structured to respond to business issues," she says. Most notably, Womack brought the objectives, goals, strategies, measures (OGSM) approach to the Capitol Hill team. As a result, "we no longer got sidetracked by the squeaky wheel, but focused on where and how we could add value." Womack argued that "every issue had a cost factor and a return of the company's investment on our effort," Hoover says. "You have to think of government relations as it impacts every aspect of your business, but you need to think of it also in terms of being a profit center, because you do add value. The beauty of P&G and of Bryce's legacy was focusing on issues while delivering success. When I became Vice President of the Washington office in 1995, I embraced the memory of Bryce and built on what Marvin initiated, being an agent of change. I told management my definition of success for our office was when a member of Congress or the current White House team would call on us to come educate them on how a bill or a policy would positively or negatively impact business." Hoover's measure of success proved true—as they dealt with tax bills, members, and staff of the House Ways and Means Committee and the Senate Finance Committee would call her office. "They would ask, 'If we implement these policies, what does this do to business? Does this hurt you or help you? What is the overall impact?' The process was a positive, educational exchange."

Hoover looks back on her office's efforts in the battle over the North American Free Trade Agreement (NAFTA) as one of its greatest achievements built on the legacy left by Harlow. Fierce opposition to the proposal centered on the fear of many lost U.S. jobs. "We thought about how to present our view to Congress on NAFTA and used creative thinking from our P&G colleagues in Packaging and in Product Supply—specifically David Elliott, also a protégé of Bryce Harlow. We developed the concept of using a Pringles can as a graphic chart to show where all product ingredients were sourced and the numbers of people both small and large employed by our suppliers as a result of Pringles." It was all about showing the family of suppliers that make Pringles successful. The Pringles "family photo" helped humanize the issue. "I know in the years after NAFTA passed, individuals who opposed it felt we lost a lot of jobs," Hoover says. "But if you look at the statistics, we gained much more than we lost. Trade agreements are good for this country and good for Procter & Gamble because they tear down barriers that keep us from selling our products on a global basis."

Hoover saw the adoption of Harlow's straightforwardness approach pay dividends in P&G's acquisition of Gillette, headquartered in Massachusetts. The late Senator Ted Kennedy was among those skeptical of the purchase. Hoover's previous contact with him had been ten years earlier when, running for office, he had been a vocal critic of P&G's closing its facility in Massachusetts. "He had been working with the union and had a great deal of misinformation," Hoover remembers. As part of a high-ranking P&G delegation, she visited the senator to put the record straight. "We talked about how long we were going to help our employees in the transitional period of finding work and providing them with outplacement, giving them the support they needed. After the Senator learned how we treated our employees, he became an advocate for us." As the Gillette deal finalized, "I reminded Senator Kennedy we were the company he had dealt with before and had been supportive of. His acceptance of the acquisition proved helpful to the overall success of this purchase."

Although, following Harlow's lead, Hoover does not tell stories that betray others' confidences, she is happy to share one that reveals her in a less-than-perfect light. It is of the day Harlow came to her and asked if she knew who Robert Redford was. "I had just seen *The Way We Were*," Hoover recalls. "And, like most women, I fantasized about meeting him." Redford, Harlow explained to Hoover, was apparently preparing to make a movie of the Watergate book, *All the President's Men*, and wanted to speak with Harlow about his time working for Nixon. Harlow wanted Hoover to do some research about Redford and then join them for the meeting. The research did not take Hoover long, but getting ready for the meeting did. "I got up at about 6 a.m. and teased my hair—big hair was in, in those days, and I piled it on top my head." Hoover put on "the tightest dress I could possibly find and applied more makeup than Alice Cooper." She finished by stepping into a pair of 6-inch stiletto pumps—only to find herself, at about 6 feet 6 inches, towering over Redford standing some 5 feet 8 inches tall. "I was totally embarrassed, plus the fact I didn't look anything like myself," Hoover admits.

"But what I remember most about this meeting was not the attire, but the discussion between Bryce and Redford. Bryce told him that Watergate reaffirmed the old truth that eternal vigilance remains the price of liberty. He talked about integrity and reiterated that in politics, one's word is one's bond. Redford heard that habitual truthtelling and square dealing are of paramount importance. If you lose your integrity, you need to leave town, which was the basis of Bryce's attempt to suggest Nixon resign. I never forgot those words. They set a framework for the remainder of my career and immortalized core values for future generations of Congress. Bryce always believed that you managed your work by doing the right thing...and if you do, then this is a very honorable profession worthy of very talented people. If you practice core values, the return on the investment to the company can be extraordinary."

4

Paul Charron

Paul Charron has proven that enduring principles transcend culture or environment, and he traces the core of the beliefs he has carried through a varied and successful business career to his early years with Procter & Gamble (P&G). The company "is a central contributor to any success I have had," says the Vietnam vet whose appointment to the helm at struggling fashion house Liz Claiborne, in 1994, surprised many who doubted a newcomer to the industry had what it would take to turn things around. But when he retired in 2006, having led the company through an extended season of sustained growth in sales, profit, and stock price, he had long silenced any naysayers. Although he had to learn the fashion world, it was only so that he could better apply the things he had already learned through more than seven years in P&G's ranks, rising from Brand Assistant on Joy dishwashing detergent to become, eventually, Brand Manager for Cheer detergent.

Charron identifies five key values being driven home during his P&G tenure: quality, integrity, responsiveness to consumer needs, analytical rigor, and commitment to mentoring. "Quality was key to everything that was done," he says. "Product quality, quality of work, quality of life." That was drilled into him in his first Brand Manager assignment for Dawn dishwashing detergent. It needed to cut grease better than any other product—requiring 50% more cleaning agents. "The product was built to be better, on dimensions that were important to the consumer," Charron says. "So quality was a critical core value."

17

Charron credits former P&G Chairman Ed Harness for an essential value he learned. He recalls hearing Harness say at a meeting, "At Procter & Gamble, we always try to do what seems about right." He says, "That was a commitment to quality of thinking, quality of execution, and most importantly, to a company of integrity. I can't tell you the number of times I've quoted Ed Harness on that."

The third core value he learned was responsiveness to consumer needs. "The whole act of brand positioning is based on an understanding of the consumer, how the product fits into her life, and how she uses the product," Charron says. "That was paramount. If you didn't have a unique reason for being that was important to the consumer, you didn't have a product; you didn't have a brand positioning. I remember hearing from one of my many bosses at P&G that the act of brand positioning is the most sacred act of brand management—that it is based on superior consumer insights, which generally means responsiveness to consumer needs."

Charron also credits P&G for emphasizing the importance of research. "From the time you became a Brand Assistant, you were doing analyses," he says. "There were share analyses, promotion analyses—you were tumbling numbers to find the absolute truths as well as the kernels of truth." All that research taught him that "judgment is a wonderful thing, but you always have to be guided by fact-based analysis and objectivity. Judgment is an enabler, it's a facilitator, but the foundation of whatever you do is based on the facts of the situation." He points to the extensive test market work that went into Dawn ahead of its national campaign. Although the product was rated highly, the P&G team found that when placed on an end cap display at the front of stores with south-facing windows, the product's color faded. Its appealing blue turned to murky gray. "The UV rays of the sun essentially took all the color out of the product. So we had to put a UV barrier into the bottle," he says, "and we wouldn't have found that out if we hadn't test marketed so thoroughly."

Charron says that the fundamental value element that mattered so much toward making the others stick was P&G's recognized commitment to mentoring, encouraging "a learning environment. That has been and continues to be central to shaping core values and affirming a company's culture." For Charron, it began "the day I walked in the door." His first Brand Manager, Gus McPhie, was "an incredible leader—bright, conscientious, and very committed to my development." There were others, too. "There was always a lesson to be learned, and they always made time to share." Some of the coaching was in formal settings, but most was just "day to day." Charron says, "It was part of a way of life that shaped me and instilled in me a 'system' that I carried with me in the various companies I had the opportunity to serve later on." Charron says of those he had the opportunity to observe up close in leadership at P&G: "It was a gift from them, so I've just followed the example."

When Charron departed P&G for bigger challenges, he packed those five value anchors into a bag in which he had brought one preexisting conviction to the company: that he could make it, if he applied himself and what he knew. Although Charron's subsequent career took him to different fields—from food, to printing, and to fashion before returning to food, becoming chairman of Campbell Soup Company in 2009—wherever he went, he "would apply the component parts of the playbook" he had studied at P&G. About his initial days when he joined Liz Claiborne, he says, "Yeah, there was a lot I didn't know, but there was a lot I did know, and much of what I had done was relevant. The 'fashionistas' focused on all the dissimilarities in my background. I wasn't really too concerned about it. I had a scheme for looking at unfamiliar territory." The P&G principles he had learned "would enlighten and inform me," he says. "It was a real blessing. Yes, I had a lot of confidence, but I had learned my lessons well. I might not have known exactly how things would end up when I came into a company, but I sure knew how to start. I knew the approach I was going to take."

I was committed to quality, I was focused on integrity and transparency in all the things we did. I believed in the consumer. I believed she would tell us the things that were important to her. I respected her for her intellect. I used the tools and analysis to get the facts, and I structured a mentoring/learning environment. All that is like 'hello.' It's basic. It becomes intuitive. I didn't have to think about this. It was reflexive because of the foundation I had."

At Liz Claiborne, Charron unpacked his P&G tool kit. "I asked a lot of questions. I conducted research. I initiated formalized planning, and I had to teach people how to do a strategic plan. I provided a context in training from the people we had." He also focused on teaching, setting up an academy-like company. The changes prompted *The Wall Street Journal* to write about "Liz Claiborne, the P&G of fashion," to which Charron said, "Yes, exactly. That's exactly what I wanted to build." He is quick to underscore that the turnaround was not achieved single-handedly. "I had an awful lot of people who were very, very good, and we worked together exceptionally well. I hired really bright people, I surrounded them with bright people, and I didn't do their jobs. I was kind of like the symphony conductor, and we all brought different gifts. That's a variation on some of the P&G things, but the foundation was pure P&G, and then the rest of the stuff was kind of what I picked up in the intervening 10 or 15 years, making a lot of mistakes."

Charron says that core values can be seen as the mercury in the barometer measuring an enterprise's temperature. "They provide the foundation," he says. "As these values are the underpinning of the enterprise, they provide the baseline as sales and profits and stock price move about. When things are going well, it's generally because people are really living and driving the core values." As a counselor to young leaders now, he says that those "rich in potential need to articulate the principles which they think will guide them as they build their career. As a CEO, your responsibility is to regenerate these core values, not to regenerate yourself." Today's newcomers sometimes seem to be in a hurry, he notes. Leaving Notre Dame for naval service, and then going to Harvard Business School, by the time he subsequently left P&G, he says, "I'd had 17 years of training before I was 37 years old. I had been living and working ever since I got out of high school, in high-quality environments, and one of the things that I tell young people is that, 'You're a rough stone; you're not a polished diamond.'" He advises young people to start with the best, most substantial company they can find. "Don't worry about starting salary; worry about the experience you'll have in three years. What will you have at the end of three years? And you want to work for someone who will care about you—someone who has sound experience and is willing to share. Those things are really critical. It doesn't matter where you start. It matters how you start, and that's with the right type of company, with the right type of supervisor, in a learning culture."

5

Cynthia Round

"Core values are not so much a script to be learned and repeated as an experience to be shared and replicated," says Cynthia Round. "They are communicated better through people than merely on paper." The principles by which she helps lead United Way in effecting change for millions in the United States and around the world were shaped and honed in her formative business years with Procter & Gamble (P&G)—and instilled largely through the encouragement and opportunities she received there. "It was more from experience than written policy," she says. It stems from the "culture of mentoring" she encountered upon arriving at the company fresh from college more than 30 years ago.

Her first assignment was a classic example of mentoring. Reporting to Joseph P. Durrett, then Brand Manager for Downy, she says, "He gave me real projects and substantive assignments, encouraging me to be innovative, to take risks and be creative." Round recalls how she would demur at first, telling Durrett she did not think that she was that creative. "He'd say, 'Sure you are,' and he would demonstrate to me how I was a creative person. He really pulled that out of me in many ways."

Another role model was Bob Wehling, the Ad Manager when Round arrived in Cincinnati as a Downy Brand Assistant. The two have reconnected in recent times as members of the advisory board of the Ad Council. "Even in his retirement," she says, "he still dedicates so much passion to the power of advertising to change the world, believing that we can galvanize people to create change. I track that back to the way I knew him as one of my first mentors and coaches."

Encouragement from the likes of Durrett and Wehling helped Round clarify and solidify values she learned growing up. She saw them mirrored in P&G's approach to business. "Ethical behavior, teamwork and collaboration, discipline, and accountability," she says. "Those things drove how we worked, and they were then very much part of the leader I became inside and outside the company. They are the kind of values that define the person I try to be, not only in my work but in my personal life."

Just how those concepts were woven into Round's outlook was clear when she left P&G after eight years. Having worked on branding for bar soap and household cleaning products, Round was chosen for a two-year assignment in Rome, helping the company launch Pampers there. On returning to the United States, she jumped ship to join advertising leaders Ogilvy & Mather, having discovered that she loved this aspect of business. For her first assignment at her new employer, she was asked to lead an account for the Kimberly-Clark Corporation—Huggies diapers. She declined, explaining that she couldn't use what she knew about Pampers marketing plans against her former employer. "I explained it would just be a real violation of my personal ethical standard," she says. That "straight up, on the table" way of approaching work she had absorbed at P&G "factored into the way I did business and have continued to work throughout my career," she says.

Her time in Rome illustrates another P&G strength: the company's willingness to invest in young talent. "It was part of the culture of mentoring, encouraging, and empowering young people to be accountable and to seize opportunity, to take risks, to make contributions," she says of the chance she was given. "I believe I was one of the first American women to be sent overseas. I asked for an international assignment and they immediately said, 'Yes, why not?' That is symbolic of the way the company nurtures and gives young people an opportunity to grow and really contribute."

Providing similar opportunities for people to contribute in different ways has driven Round's work as Executive Vice President, Brand Leadership at United Way Worldwide. She joined the nonprofit—the world's largest—after 15 years with Ogilvy & Mather (O&M), but her awareness of United Way stretched back to her P&G days. "I was first introduced to United Way at P&G, became a donor and supporter, and was keenly aware of the company's strong support for it," she recalls. Although it was later that she was invited to sit on various nonprofit boards, the giving back "was part of my foundational Procter experience." The circle has since been completed, with Round now working closely with Jorge Uribe, President of P&G Latin America, who is a member of the United Way Worldwide board. The two are closely involved in taking the charity's Born Learning initiative to encourage early childhood education across Latin America.

Round has found the principles that guided her in business to be invaluable in "trying to mobilize people for the common good as opposed to toward the purchase of a product or service" at United Way. The basics transcend the cultural gap between for-profit and nonprofit, just as she found they did when she swapped P&G America for its Italian operation. Living in Rome was "a little bit more chaotic, a little bit more crazy" than the young woman raised in rural Oklahoma was used to, but at work the core values were "very much the same: The day-to-day work ethic that was there, the fact-based, kind of collegial teamwork-oriented approach. That kind of spirit was very much in common with what I had experienced in Cincinnati."

Round has had to draw on her P&G and O&M experiences as "brand steward" for United Way as it has faced two tests in recent years—redefining its place and role in an increasingly crowded world of charitable endeavors. Founded 125 years ago, United Way has long been almost synonymous with charitable giving in the United States.

Round calls it "an icon of American philanthropy." With more than 1,200 local United Ways across country, the charity raises around $4 billion a year, enjoying 95% brand awareness. One in four Americans donates to the cause. But today there are almost 1.3 million nonprofits in the United States. "It's a huge sector," Round says. "And so marketing, share of mind, and share of wallet apply just as much as they do in the business world." Round found herself "very well prepared by my P&G experience and from working in many different categories at Ogilvy around the world, to create a positive brand experience, build and sustain more personal relationships with supporters, and retain relevancy of a 125-year-old brand."

In addition to the growing competition from other charitable causes for people's compassion, United Way found that it faced another challenge. Though it was extremely well known, most people had only a vague sense of what United Way stood for. "Though everyone would say that United Way does 'good things,' very few could tell us what it actually did," says Round. At the same time, the charity's leaders acknowledged that although people were being generous and the nonprofit sector was raising more and more money, "the social problems in this country weren't getting better." That twin realization led to Round's part in refocusing the charity's efforts in three areas: education, income, and health, the building blocks of quality of life. In 2008, United Way announced 10-year bold Goals for the Common Good to help dramatically cut the dropout rate in education, reduce the number of financially unstable families, and increase general health in adults and children. This focus has helped reinvigorate the charity's support base, says Round. "People needed to know more about the specifics, the work behind the brand that they trusted and invested in." For many years, she observes, "the goal of American philanthropy was how much money can we raise and contribute to good causes...We needed a different strategy, greater focus—to be measuring not how much money we raise, but how are we changing lives?"

As a result, United Way shifted to "community impact, really trying to move the needle on social problems and not being satisfied with how much money we raise or how many volunteers we recruit. Rather, we ask, 'Are we actually changing things?' It's certainly changing our business, our focus, and the impact that we can make. And I think it's changing the sector in the USA and around the world."

Round acknowledges that there are areas where the nonprofit sector does operate a little differently from the business world. One is when it comes to goal setting. "Visioning is a very important part of setting a goal," she says. "One of the things about 10 years is it's far enough to be able to think really big and yet not so close as you have to have everything worked out exactly. You have to know more precisely how you're going to hit a three-year goal." United Way's Goals for the Common Good are ambitious: halving dropout rates and the number of financially unstable families and increasing by a third the number of adults and kids measurably improving their health. "When we set those goals in 2008, we couldn't say that we knew exactly how we were going to make it, but we challenged America to work together across business, government, and nonprofit sectors to reach for this kind of significant social change. "I do believe it was the right thing to set these aspirational goals, because it is mobilizing and galvanizing people toward something that seems important, though possible. Even if we fall short of the specific targets, we will have achieved more by reaching high."

Having flourished through mentoring, Round looks for opportunities to offer a similar boost to young people as a board member of the Advertising Educational Foundation. On campuses, "I tell them my P&G story, giving them encouragement to follow their dreams, to manage their own destiny, and to find and choose people they trust and from whom they can learn. In order to grow, you need to seek those kinds of mentors as a young person. Then you need to become one of those mentors when you get inside and have a job. It was critical in my own personal journey that my first job was with P&G. In those formative years, core values and mentoring shape the kind of person you're going to become. I had the gift of those people to encourage, build, and challenge me to become the best person and professional that I could be."

6

John Smale

John Smale, former Procter & Gamble (P&G) CEO and former Chairman of the Board for General Motors, is both a leader and a historian. Smale's speech to the Commonwealth Commercial Club in 1993 represents leadership driven by core values. He said, "As I look out, I see faces of many, many friends. People that I've known, respected, and admired for decades and those of you that make up the leadership of Cincinnati working hard to make this city an attractive place to live. Your backgrounds and the organizations you've helped lead are all unique, of course, but you've shared the responsibilities of leadership. You've all grappled with the nebulous, but crucial challenge of shaping a vision and then guiding an organizational structure and culture that stimulates people to contribute their full potential to a common objective. I guess that's my own definition of leadership: shaping a vision and then trying to ensure that the organization has all the tangible as well as intangible qualities needed to attain and preserve that vision. And in this process of attaining a vision, I suspect that you would agree with me that there is one axiom that will remain true regardless of how fast the marketplace, technology, and society itself may change. That axiom is that people, not physical assets, are any organization's most valuable resource.

"But, judging from the unprecedented events that have shaken one company after another in recent years—IBM, General Motors, Kodak, Sears, Westinghouse, American Express, and on and on—managements seem to have more and more difficulty keeping focused on a vision that is not only attainable, but sustainable. As I've been exposed to those events—some of them by close involvement—I've come to wrestle more and more in my own mind with two questions: What causes so many great companies to lose their industry dominance and leadership; and how, realistically, might these failures have been avoided?

"Let me share an example of what I think is one of the most remarkable instances of institution gaining, losing, and then regaining leadership. The year was 1943, and the United States Army had yet to be tested in combat against the Germans. When the confrontation finally came, at the Kasserine Pass in western Tunisia, the Americans fled. The Commander-in-Charge of the Allied forces, Dwight Eisenhower, immediately authorized General George Patton to shake up the American field command. The first commander Patton relieved was the general who had been in charge at the Kasserine Pass: the very general who Eisenhower himself had rated as his best commander after Patton. Eisenhower had no qualms about demoting his old friend, nor did his boss George Marshall, or the man on the spot, Patton. Boldness and swiftness were understood to be the order of the day. The stakes were nothing less than survival. Less than two years after the debacle at the Kasserine Pass, the American army was respected universally as the most powerful and effective military organization ever amassed.

"Another twenty years later, however, that same army was suffering from what the historian Neil Sheehan calls 'the disease of victory.' The junior officers who had begun their careers under the Marshalls, Eisenhowers, and Pattons had become so accustomed to victory and dominance after the end of World War II that they perceived very little need to question the institution's view of the world or its doctrine, its structure, or culture. Unlike the mindset of Eisenhower, Marshall, and Patton in 1943, the mind-set of this army had no pace for the possibility of losing a battle or a war anywhere in the world, let alone in a country as small and isolated as Vietnam. What were often referred to as the 'three Ms'—men, money, and material—were the accepted tools needed to maintain dominance. It was assumed that there would never be a lack of any one of them. Jump forward another ten years, and that same peerless army [was] in the throes of unprecedented criticism and doubt from within and without as the world witnessed the evacuation of Saigon.

"Now, today, that army has, in a sense, come full circle. Officers who started their careers under the commanders of the Fifties and Sixties learned the lessons of arrogance and complacency firsthand. And, they applied those lessons when their turn came at the reins of leadership. Commanding officers like Colin Powell and Norman Schwarzkopf were much more akin to the mind-set of the Eisenhowers and Pattons of World War II than the one of the Westmorelands and Harkinses of Vietnam. As a result, the U.S. Army has regained its pride, nimbleness, and effectiveness.

"All organizations—business as well as social—go through similar cycles. Indeed, it happens to countries and to civilizations. Success breeds failure unless deliberate steps are taken to avoid it. What determines whether an organization rejuvenates itself after its leadership is threatened (or whether it even realizes the threat until it's too late) is a matter of individual leadership style and focus as well as the organization's culture. Failure—that is, loss of leadership—doesn't occur overnight. It occurs over a period of many, many years. The failure may not be apparent in a company's financial results until near the final crisis, but any careful examination of a company that's lost its leadership will show the root of failure was there years and years before the failure became evident in the results. And, such examination will show that it need not have occurred. There are very few 'Acts of God' behind these failures. The fault is not in the stars. It is in ourselves.

"There are really three aspects of industry leadership: intellectual leadership (vision), capability leadership, and results leadership.

1. The company that becomes the intellectual leader is the one that sets the direction of the industry itself through conceptual innovation—a new way to think about a market, its products, and customer desires. Examples are what Alfred Sloan did in the auto industry; what George Eastman did with photography; what IBM did with computers in the 1960s; what Bill Gates has done with computer software in the 1990s; and indeed what Procter & Gamble did with the concept of brand marketing in the 1930s.

   Each of these companies came forth with a new vision of the product and how the customer wanted to use it. Their vision was radically different from established tenants and practices. They were perhaps seen as brash upstarts in the eyes of rivals of their day, but they ended up forcing the established leaders to either adapt or give us their leadership.

2. Next is capability leadership. It is a matter of ability as opposed to vision. The capability leader of an industry is the company that develops an edge in product design, manufacturing, or marketing. That edge, in turn, becomes the standard by which all competitors are measured. The capability leader is the company all competitors strive to match. It's the company you look at when you are benchmarking your own company's capabilities.

   Henry Ford and the early years of his Ford Motor Company are a prime example. Ford's methods of mass production redefined the basis of competition for several decades. Now, the advent of lean and agile manufacturing processes, which are still evolving, has redefined the basis of competition.

   This also happened in retailing. Sears, with its network of sprawling mall stores, became the benchmark by which all retailers measured themselves in the 1960s, but the advent of upscale specialty stores, deep-discounters, and stores based on the concept of everyday low prices has since redefined the basis of competition again.

3. The third aspect of leadership is results leadership. It is the art of putting all elements of vision and capability together to produce superior results on the bottom line—market share, profitability, cash flow, and return on investment. It is the most visible aspect of leadership and probably the most tangibly rewarding.

"Alfred Sloan laid the foundation that enabled the General Motors of his day to achieve leadership in all three areas: intellectual, capability, and results. His company's intellectual leadership stemmed from his revolutionary initial vision—the concept of 'a car for every purse and purpose,' which was the antithesis of Henry Ford's approach of offering his customers any color of car they wanted as long as it was black. Sloan's capability leadership was tied to that vision: a full product line with clearly differentiated nameplates. His company's offerings in each segment of the market had a unique brand name and image apart from General Motors itself. At the same time, his company was the one that constantly refined the product itself with such innovations as the electric starter, the closed body, the radio, and automatic transmission. Finally, Sloan achieved results leadership by being able to attain and sustain the lowest breakeven level of any competitor. He did this through constant innovation in technology and marketing as well as his famous vertically integrated network of parts and vehicle assembly operations. But, despite his organization's success, he was well aware of the fragile and temporal nature of leadership in a competitive world. This is what he said when he published his memoirs in 1963. It has proven to be both prophetic and ironic.

"Growth and progress are related, for there is no resting place for an enterprise in a competitive economy. Obstacles, conflicts, new problems in various shapes, and new horizons arise to stir the imagination and continue the progress of industry. Success, however, may bring self-satisfaction. In that event, the urge for competitive survival, the strongest of economic incentives, is dulled. The spirit of venture is lost in the inertia of the mind against change. When such influences develop, growth may be arrested or a decline may set in, caused by the failure to recognize advancing technology or altered consumer needs, or perhaps by competition that is more virile or aggressive.

"The perpetuation of an unusual success or maintenance of an unusually high standard of leadership in any industry is sometimes more difficult than the attainment of that success or leadership in the first place. This is the greatest challenge to be met by the leader of the industry. Again, the fault is not in the stars, but in ourselves. When a company achieves a long period of sustained dominance, the human factors of pride, arrogance, and complacency seem to overtake many more noble qualities:

- Bureaucracy seems to replace a spirit of entrepreneurialism, and the size and complexity of the bureaucracy grow disproportionately with the growth of the business itself.

- Momentum is mistaken for leadership. Managers keep following the same strategies that once led to industry leadership long after these strategies have become invalid.

- Individual efforts become focused internally rather than externally, with more and more emphasis on internal processes and detailed analytical reports and presentations—and less emphasis on interaction with the customer and less urgency in anticipating and responding to changes in the competitive arena. In that environment, it becomes possible for a manager to know more about the art of analysis and presentation than about the business itself and still rise through the organization—even as the environment in which the business competes undergoes fundamental change.

"The philosophy that 'we can solve the problem or meet the challenge because we are rich'—the equivalent of the military's 'three Ms' of men, money, and material in the 1960s—replaces the willingness to confront new challenges not with resources but with new approaches or a new vision. And, managers who are otherwise too self-motivated to propose or initiate bold new marketplace projects or initiatives conclude that following the established pattern—continuing to do things the way they were done in the past—is the way to get ahead.

"Very few, if any, great companies develop all of these faults; but even fewer avoid developing at least some of them. The faults develop so slowly over time the organization doesn't realize it is happening. When these faults come to dominate the decision-making process, also without the organization really realizing what's happened, failure is inevitable, even if not immediate. The once-great leader is suddenly vulnerable to competitors—maybe a brash upstart who reacts with new vision and nimbleness as technologies, consumer desires, and the competitive arena itself undergo change. And, of course, that successful brash upstart will, in all likelihood, eventually be susceptible to the very faults that overcame the former leader. These thoughts lead to the second question in my inner wrestling match: How can an industry leader avoid falling victim to the cycle and preserve its leadership? There is, of course, no simple formula.

"Certainly, a clear definition and understanding of the vision throughout the organization is essential, as is a clear understanding of the capabilities required for fulfilling the vision. Crucial is management's understanding of change and its willingness to take the risks that change can often represent, particularly to the leader. There is indeed no magic formula for avoiding the loss of industry leadership once it is achieved. If the test of the brash upstart's mettle is how he or she brings innovation to such momentous crises as the debacle of Kasserine Pass, then the established leader's test is whether he or she can recognize the next Kasserine Pass over the horizon before the enemy has already lain the decisive ambush. As Aristotle said more than 2000 years ago, 'Whom the gods want to destroy, they send forty years of success.' The challenge for the great companies that are the backbone of America's competitiveness in today's interdependent world is to escape that fate."

Part II
Applying Core Values for Capability

7

Daniela Riccardi

Daniela Riccardi had been the CEO of Diesel for only a few months when she was asked about her 25 years of Procter & Gamble (P&G) experience, leading different businesses.

She says, "It's not easy to summarize, in any form, what I had learned in those 25 years. It's a lifetime and so full of learning and turning points. P&G was my first and only job until leaving for Diesel. I had just graduated from political science and international studies for a diplomatic career. Yet I was going to be a Brand Assistant on Ariel, one of the leading detergents in Italy. I remember I couldn't understand a word of what I was supposed to do—shipment analysis, share summary, deep dive in habits and practices. What was all that? I do know all of that now, and much of what I learned I have been teaching to young guys and gals who, the same as me years before, are living the amazing experience of going from their school desks to running some of the biggest brands and business in the world."

Leaving P&G came hard. Riccardi says, "It was not easy to quit P&G after so many years, but fashion had always been one of my big passions, and after a quarter of a century with P&G, I decided that the jump was now or never. Many people asked me what detergents and diapers, hair care, and beauty creams had to do with fashion. More than what people think. And, early on in my new job I realized, in fact, that what I learned in those 25 years was to apply principles and criteria that are, and will remain, valid and valuable in any country, culture, business, and category."

Diesel is a 33-year-old successful fashion global brand that has grown year after year and today is one of the most iconic lifestyle brands. Renzo Rosso, the founder and owner of the company, is a 55-year-old man—"an inspiring, creative visionary and an extremely smart businessman," Riccardi says. "When he created Diesel, he wanted to make of it 'the casual alternative to luxury.' And that's what Diesel is today for its fans, spread across every single corner of the world."

The brand allure and character are summarized in two phrases often found in the products and in their advertising: "Diesel for successful living" and "Only the brave." "This is the essence of the brand," she says, "its strategic and unique positioning and what I realized, early on, was the biggest and most valuable asset of the entire company. This is the first principle I learned from P&G and brought with me. There is no business potential in a company without a powerful brand; therefore, the importance of a meaningful and relevant brand equity and positioning, and the religious conviction that every element and expression of the brand needs to be coherent and consistent with its equity and DNA, is vital. This sometimes was being challenged and twisted at Diesel, where the velocity of the industry and volatility of the fashion world impose continuous updates. But a meaningful, distinctive, and relevant positioning is ageless. I got this lesson very clearly in my early days at P&G when, like every young Brand Assistant, I wanted to refresh the positioning and the look of the brand, to design a new logo, and to change the advertising campaign. I was stopped a few times by veterans of the brand, who taught me that the positioning of a brand is a picture of its identity and should never be changed. And I had been teaching this relentlessly to my people in P&G and to those at Diesel now: Never change the positioning that made the brand famous, and remember that most likely it is the reason people still buy the brand. In fact, in difficult or uncertain times, the best thing to do is to build on the strengths of a brand, on its heritage, its purpose, and its reason for being. That by itself enhances the value of the brand."

She went on: "The second important thing I learned as a core value of P&G that I brought with me to Diesel is the importance of product innovation. It might not look obvious what type of product innovation there can be in a pair of jeans or a leather jacket. Is there any technology and research there? There is, in fact! And it is one of the reasons why people pay up to 500 dollars for one pair of Diesel jeans—because they are made of the best denim fabric, are treated with multiple washes, and other sophisticated and innovative techniques. Each season they propose innovative silhouettes and fits, amazing branded details, trims, hardware, and improbable mixed materials. Diesel's ability to do this in a cool and fashionable way through the years has granted to Diesel the image of one of the best and most innovative companies in the casual wear industry."

Riccardi says, "Another core value that I carried with me, from my earliest P&G days in Italy to China and then to Diesel, is to keep the consumer at the center of the equation. We all serve consumers, whatever industry we work for. When I arrived at Diesel, I realized that there were many discussions about what competitors were doing, which was sometimes accompanied by an attitude just to follow the latest trend. Nobody mentioned the words 'consumer' or 'shopper.' Together with my team, we worked to put our consumers, and what they want and expect from Diesel, at the center of the equation. We have done this particularly when we are designed our female collections, and it's been no surprise that the outcome is a much stronger and very successful product offer."

As she sees it, "Obsessive branding, product innovation, and a consumer-centric culture are, in my opinion, some of the key reasons for the long-term success of P&G. I have no doubt they will be key to the future success of Diesel and of any company and brand."

What about culture, people, and organization? She says, "I grew up in a company with a very strong culture built in almost 200 years of history, around core values. The biggest and most important core value is people. All the culture of the company pivots on hiring, developing, and promoting the best talent in a system largely based on the promotion-from-within practice. Recalling debates on whether promotion from within was good or bad, I am now convinced that the practice of this principle is an extremely important aspect to preserve values, to spread them, and to build heritage from your own DNA. Our 33-year-old Diesel brand derives its values and strengths from the brand artistry and values of Renzo Rosso. Preserving and growing that artistry and those brand values is vital to the future of the brand. This is one of the reasons why, at Diesel, we are trying to implement more and more promotion from within. Beyond the advantages of speed of learning and acting versus bringing talent in from the outside, promotion from within is another important way of developing our own leadership, by personally taking on the responsibility of supporting, coaching, and guiding the men and women who will lead the brands and companies to the next level. This is, I believe, one of the most important duties of leaders."

She adds, "I would miss the most important assets of what I brought with me if I did not talk about the leadership culture of P&G and of two lessons that I found myself using most in the 25 years at P&G, and probably the ones that I treasure most now as CEO at Diesel: Leading by Principles and Always Do the Right Thing. I think these two short sentences are the essence of leadership. They are lighthouses in the difficult moments. They are eternal and transcend cultures, business, and any type of boundaries. I consider them among the key heritages that make P&G proud of exporting talent to other companies. I recall hearing then-CEO A.G. Lafley being asked how he felt about losing so many great leaders in the company, who departed for new challenges and opportunities elsewhere. He was sad to see them go, he said, but he was happy to know they were helping shape the future of other industries and nations. I kept on thinking about those words, and I think I am privileged to have an opportunity to teach others and to spread in other companies some of the best managing and leadership behaviors of any company. Leading by Principle is the acid test of leadership. It is the heavy weight that leaders need to be able to carry, to sit in a position that guides and inspires their organizations. It means having professional and ethical principles and [following] them even when not easy, unpractical, or unpopular."

"Leading by Principles goes hand in hand with Always Do the Right Thing," she says. "It's a lesson that proved invaluable to me in any of the jobs I had in my 25 years at P&G and in any of the countries I crossed, from Colombia to Russia to China. No matter how complicated or difficult the situation, whether it was a bomb threat in the office or an order from the Government to pull hundreds of millions of products from the shelves, I looked at myself in the mirror and repeated: 'Always Do the Right Thing—what's right for the business, for our customers, and for the company.' It always worked. I looked at myself in the mirror many times in my first few months at Diesel, when the culture around me [was] new and different or the business issues unusual. Again and again, Lead by Principles and Always Do the Right Thing worked and helped me to find the right path. I am coaching this now to my people—to learn and become aware of the weight and responsibility of leaders and of leading by example."

Riccardi spent her last five years with P&G leading the company operations in China. "That experience," she says, "not only taught me about applying principles to a new culture, but also increased my awareness of the importance of thinking futuristically. Working in one of the world's fastest growing economies, we had to learn to move a full step ahead of other countries, especially in the beauty sector. From my experience in China, where I witnessed close-up culture and commercial sectors leapfrogging to the forefront of change, I learned to operate by thinking that, in China, 'Today is already tomorrow.'

The Chinese consumers are ahead of the game. Their expectation on service, on products, on fashion are all ahead of the game. Western thinking frames the future as an evolution of the past, but in China, this doesn't apply. They have gone from having no telephones to having the most sophisticated mobile phones distributed to 85% of the Chinese population. It's the same with the Internet, or shopping online, same as fast trains, airports—with infrastructure of any type. From not knowing what fashion was, because they were using uniforms all made of the same fabric and cut, they have gone to being the most advanced fashion market in the world and the biggest luxury market in world. P&G had spent 20 years trying to serve the Chinese consumer the most affordable products, being sensitive to the low income level of the Chinese consumers."

"But China moved fast, and in the 20 years in which P&G had operated in China, consumer usage and habits had developed even faster. Already in most of the big cities consumers are far more savvy, sophisticated, and demanding than consumers in Western Europe or the USA, particularly in respect to beauty and fashion. The big lesson there was that thinking futuristically does not mean assuming that what we learned in the past is good for the future, particularly in China. Many of the business models and principles I had learned in the past, even after so many years of experience in developing markets, did not apply to China. Business models had to be reevaluated every two or three years, and we had to redesign them. We had to look at the future, to the needs and aspirations of the young generations that are so different in so many aspects from their parents. We had to look at the technological development of the country, which is advanced enough to allow an incredibly rapid knowledge growth, the fastest ever use of information, and China to be at the heart of global networking. Leading P&G in China was an invaluable experience for me, another amazing chapter of my growth as business leader and as an individual—a very timely one, now that Diesel is preparing for a significant expansion in China."

As she puts it, "I listened for many years to the leaders of P&G talking about the importance of core values. More than ever, I now understand how that was true. They are a gift, and to keep them alive, to bring them to other companies and communities for the enlightenment of the next generations is a duty and responsibility. We can only contribute that way to create a better business environment and hopefully a better world."

8

Wolfgang Berndt

For Wolfgang Berndt, living a culture of trusts has made all the difference. After 34 years with Procter & Gamble (P&G), retiring as President of P&G Europe, Middle East, Africa as well as Global Fabric & Home Care, he fondly recalls his second day with the company that forever changed his own core values. "Claude Salomon, the manager who has just interviewed and hired me, was scheduled in a meeting in Geneva, Switzerland. As Claude is leaving the office he said, 'Here are the keys to the office and my desk drawer. You can see all the files except in the bottom two.'" Berndt felt so honored by this trust and was indelibly changed by the experience. His application of this core value became one of the most durable leadership traits, especially as P&G grew in international markets. "When trust is an inherent element of the organization's culture, people will typically respond by raising their own internal performance expectations, personal accountability, and sense of ownership. As a core value, trust is liberating, and it naturally leads to doing whatever it takes to meet or exceed the requirements of the job. Often that means coming up with creative solutions and shaping new approaches to succeed in foreign lands."

The success of Berndt and his global teams would require internal trust, risk taking, and strategic insight. In three and a half decades, his teams created a consumer packaged goods business from scratch in Eastern Europe and penetrated the Middle East, Africa, and Latin America. During the seven years he was heading up the Latin American business and the seven years he led the company's entry into Eastern Europe and the former Soviet Union, his teams more than doubled P&G's footprint in Latin America and created market-leading consumer packaged goods businesses across a large number of categories in the reforming economies of the previous Soviet bloc. Changing the company's strategic approach from geographic to regional and global was a key requisite in making this work in such a short time.

In 1988, Berndt suggested to then-CEO John Smale that the company should start to educate themselves in Eastern Europe. Shaping their strategy in a disciplined manner, Berndt's team began to gather information from local politicians about the pending new governments. Rallying around new ideals, P&G and a new neighborhood of surrounding, noncompeting countries began to embrace free market thinking. Poland, Czechoslovakia, and Hungary were particularly eager to jettison past frustrations in pursuit of free market enterprise.

One of the challenges P&G faced in these countries was that Unilever, Henkel, and state-owned regional competitors already had a foothold with manufacturing facilities in most of these countries. Unilever and Henkel's perspective was that manufacturing could go the way of many developing countries in Latin America and Asia should communism end. At the time, high-import barriers forced local production of consumer-packaged goods, including soap and paper-based products. "The problem with this approach, however, was that the multitude of small local plants was inefficient to operate, difficult, and expensive to upgrade for new technology leading to product improvements. This environment led to higher-priced product to the end consumer."

During meetings with the new, market-oriented political leaders in these countries, Berndt and his team realized that Poland, Czechoslovakia, and Hungary were unlikely to go this way because they recognized the benefit of open markets. Accordingly, the P&G team came up with a regional, rather than country-by-country, strategy.

The central idea was to create world-class plants in terms of size, quality, and costs, which could serve whole regions.

Following this approach, laundry product manufacturing was established in an upgraded and expanded plant in Rakovnik, Czech Republic; a diaper plant was established in Poland, and Health & Beauty Aids/Feminine Hygiene Manufacturing was located in Hungary. This strategy provided a broad P&G array of product for distribution across all of Eastern Europe at a significantly lower price to consumers. There was plenty of forethought about the strategy. The P&G team anticipated change, recognized market conditions, identified cultural differences, capitalized on an exploding free market, and influenced local leaders to embrace their multilateral production strategy without material effect to local labor, all while using lessons from their exploits in Latin America. Aided by brand strategy that focused on a new generation of consumers, P&G tapped into a population hungry for western quality product. Backed by advertising with consistent taglines used in each television commercial about product quality, the traditional P&G model to reach consumers with a brand promise hit the airwaves. And understanding that free product was never a part of the communist culture, significant sampling of product created new trial usage.

It was a seminal moment in consumer packaged goods history. The intersection of a free market with P&G quality along with the unionization of the European community was a once-in-a-lifetime event. To bolster their team effort, ambassadors of the new culture were moved into Eastern Europe. These were current P&G employees born in Poland, Hungary, or Czech who had a special affinity for their country. Along with many great additions from Latin America, the backbone for long-term success was established. An empowered team of P&G professionals filled leadership roles in production, logistics, operations, brand management, and sales. And they were out to change the world of consumer package goods.

Similar to Latin America, the new teams used their "metabolic speed" as a defensible strategy for fast expansion. Unlike North America, global teams were often under-resourced and often did not have all the data available to analyze their markets. Berndt's teams had a "burning passion to win with less emphasis on finding reasons to not move fast on initiatives. Our motor simply ran at a different RPM than the rest of the world," he says. "Consistent with company core values, we were disciplined, focused, and aligned to succeed. It was down to every single individual working on the right agenda, rolling out initiatives that could be achieved with greater, faster success rates. With supreme force and focus, P&G brands were getting higher consumer acceptance rates while our plants were producing higher quality, innovative products at lower costs. In military fashion, we grew market share, profits increased, and shareholder values consistently grew, all on the back of a team that had trust at the center of its culture."

9

Mike Clasper

Individual personality is an important part of leadership, but it is most fruitful when it's matched with shared principles. Call it the "me-plus-we" equation. That balance epitomizes the varied careers of Mike Clasper, who credits that formula to his 20-plus successful years with Procter & Gamble (P&G), despite being a non-American who never served time stateside in the organization.

The critical need for a marriage of vision and values became clear to Clasper when he was appointed Head of Global Homecare for P&G. All his prior experience had been in Europe. He assumed the global role, convinced of the need for a broad view of the business. These, he knew, may "not necessarily be the best decisions for the American homecare business if making that decision means that collectively our costs go up or a product development cycle time goes out." It was "a really tough start," he recalls. "Why should they listen to somebody who's got this funny accent, from another part of the world?" But he says, "the great thing is that the P&G principles"—fundamentally, doing the best by the consumer and doing that the right way—"got us miles past that." So much so that, by the time Clasper departed the post and the company in 2001, there were tears in Cincinnati from the team he had led from his UK base.

Since leaving P&G, Clasper has held high-profile positions as the head of the BAA PLC, a British-based airports company, and since 2008 he has acted as the Chairman of Her Majesty's Revenue & Customs, which oversees for the government tax collection and benefit payments. There and in his other leadership positions, both in business and the public sector, he has, he says, "constantly taken things from my P&G past and placed them in the new places I have gone to." He drew on P&G's famed objectives, goals, strategies, measures (OGSM) approach at BAA and elsewhere. At the airports company, he had to explain to customer British Airways (BA) how his organization was now approaching strategic deployment issues. "As we work together, we might want to look at doing something similar together," he recalls telling them in a low-key way. Clasper was astonished when the BA people told him they were doing something similar, because "we had a guy from P&G in here and we adopted it." For Clasper, the exchange was a classic example of P&G's widespread, quiet influence. "There's no better one than to find the leading airport and the leading airline in the UK talking to each other and they find out they're both using something that was derived from OGSMs that came from people who were in P&G."

Clasper recalls P&G's discipline and focus being modeled for him from his early days with the company. He joined not long before the Rely tampon crisis brought unwanted headlines but, later, widespread admiration for the way the company swiftly pulled the product from the market. "Later, when I was in a more senior position having to make some decisions, it was easy to make the right decision, because you knew where the values were," he says of the company's Rely course of action. That time came for Clasper when P&G introduced Ariel liquid in the UK. Without a strong market share in the country, the company needed a runaway success to overtake competitor Unilever. The new product tested well, he says, and "was already starting to be a roaring success, when we discovered that we had a quality problem, just as we had scaled up."

The company knew about the quality problem, but retailers were demanding more supplies than P&G could provide, even ignoring the quality issues and running full bore. "We got one of those national, word-of-mouth type effects...the stuff was running away twice as fast as we thought it would be," Clasper said. "So the issue was, do we not tell anybody we've got a product problem, leave it in the trade, let it drift out to consumers, and thereby fuel this success without risking the retailer relationship, or even have customers going into stores and not being able to find the product? Or do we pull the product that we know is faulty and, in fact, slow down a very, very successful launch—and get a lot of retailers really mad, because the one thing a retailer doesn't want when he's got a runaway success is not to have the product." The decision "was easy," he says. "We only had one choice. The product wasn't to the right quality, so we took it out of the trade, and then we worked night and day to make sure that we got back to where we should have been."

The launch lost momentum, of course, and money—the sputter cost millions of dollars, Clasper estimates. But P&G did eventually go on to overtake Unilever's market share despite the stall. Clasper calls the decision "one of the most important things that the UK company did while I was Marketing Director. At the time that you made the decision, you didn't know what was going to happen; you were risking the launch, but you were clear that you couldn't leave product that wasn't of the right quality out there—you had to bring it back." This was not a decision of Rely proportions, involving health concerns, he recognizes—but it was perhaps just as significant an example of principled decision-making. "It was basically a cleaning performance problem. It wasn't something that everybody would have found. This wasn't toxic shock syndrome, but it was values in action, decision-making that many other companies would have agonized over. We just knew what we had to do, so we did it."

Clasper also found a valuable lesson in P&G's performance stumble around the turn of the millennium, when the business was widely acknowledged to have lost its way for a while and shares prices fell dramatically. Clasper looks back and blames poor leadership for the drop. The resulting recovery, led by then-chairman A.G. Lafley, he credits to "going back to P&G basic principles; the discipline, the transparency, the let's focus not on internal battles but let's focus on the retailer and the consumer. All of those got us back on track, so everybody had a line of sight to the fact that we had a brand and a product that would be used by a consumer and that internal customers and internal barriers and internal politics had to get out of the way. We just went back to the focus on the consumer and on our brands."

Reflecting on his P&G years, Clasper appreciates not just that the company had clear values but that it provided an environment in which people were put in positions where they needed to exercise those values. Placed in small teams and given responsibility early on, "you really were running the business," he says. "Obviously it's not chaos. There were some...controls around you. But there was that sense that you were responsible for the success of the business, relatively from day one. In a couple years, I had been promoted to Brand Manager and I genuinely felt I was running a significant multimillion dollar business. I had a lot of decisions that I was expected to make. It's a very empowering environment to join, and I don't think it changed in all the time that I was at P&G. You get some very young people who are made to feel that they own the business and it's their job to make it successful, and they are given a massive amount of space to do it. That contrasts with almost every other organization that I've been involved with since."

Clasper found an affinity with P&G when he arrived. Having qualified as an engineer, he'd had a brief period with British Rail, the UK's nationalized rail service. But he was "disappointed by the work ethic there: Do as little as you could get away with." Raised by the owner of a construction company who had promoted to his children the old-fashioned virtue of "a fair day's pay for a fair day's work, a really strong work ethic," Clasper found what he was looking for at P&G—"somewhere I could practice some of those values that my father had instilled in me, but on a bigger scale than a 30-people small firm in a small corner of England."

"Innovation doesn't end with achievement," Clasper says after more than 30 years in business. "It just looks different." He recalls his time as General Manager of P&G's interests in Holland—where he was literally in the shadow of market leader Unilever, whose world headquarters could be seen from P&G's modest two-floor office suite. "They were huge in Holland." But, over time, P&G chipped away to become the market leader in laundry. "We did it by having a very disruptive, innovative approach to product type," Clasper explains. "We bet the farm on liquid products, on compact products, because they fit the environmentally conscious culture of the Dutch and we went for it. I will always be proud of that; from a principles point of view, we had a very clear, strategic plan, and then we executed it with courage."

Fast-forward some, and Clasper is General Manager in the UK, where Pampers enjoys about 60% of the disposable diaper market. Kimberly-Clark breaks ground for a new factory to introduce Huggies. "Most organizations would assume that if the best worldwide competitor in the diaper market decides to enter the UK market, they are going to lose market share, right?" he says. "You start thinking, how can we reduce the effect on this so that we don't lose too much market share and so on?" But, along with Category Manager John Bennett, Clasper decided that P&G was not going to give up a single point of market share. "It was a pretty outrageous objective," he acknowledges. The team came up with a plan to grow market share ahead of Huggies' arrival, and to win back lost users afterward. "The phrase was, 'We'll not lose one single diaper,'" he says. "And we achieved it. It was a stunningly focused team effort driven by an outrageous objective, but one that we just decided we would do. I'm proud of the people who did it because, in order to do that, you can imagine the amount of innovation that was required."

Clasper's varied experiences in the years following his departure from P&G have given him insights into why and how P&G's emphasis on internal promotion works so well there and may be as effective elsewhere. He considers the approach a core part of the company's strength, "because it both encourages and motivates somebody to know that if they are the best that they can be, there's not somebody who's going to appear from somewhere way out in left field who is going to get the promotion away from them. It creates a real sense of encouragement to strive to get to the top. I think it has massive advantages in that people grow up with a set of values, so you know, there are certain almost automatic responses that make doing business as a relatively junior member of the team at P&G much easier than in many other organizations." The potential downside is the danger of "group think—where everybody's agreeing, but it's the wrong answer," he comments. This Achilles' heel is tempered in P&G's case, though, by its place in the fast-moving world of consumer goods, Clasper believes. "If group think occurs, the market tells you very quickly that you've got it wrong." But "if you're making, let's say, an aircraft—to take one of my later experiences—then, you don't know you've got it wrong in market share terms for ten years after you start the project."

10

Ed Rigaud

Although Ed Rigaud was a rare African American in Procter & Gamble's (P&G's) ranks when he arrived in 1965, he recognized early on another kind of diversity, that "of thought and style." He leaned on those strengths through a successful 35-year-plus career with the company and later with his key leadership role in the founding of the landmark National Underground Railroad Freedom Center (NURFC), the Cincinnati museum and education center founded to trace and honor efforts to abolish slavery and to apply those lessons today. "We're trying to take that spark that's inside of most folks and turn it into a flame, and inspire them and challenge them," Rigaud says of the project, "so they will take courageous steps for freedom today."

The leadership he brought to the nine-year task of establishing the center drew on the diversity epitomized in P&G's product development process. He was the first African American appointed a Director of Product Development, and says, "We would put together a packaging team, a product delivery team, we actually called it, diverse thinkers—people who were analytical, people who were strong in synthesis or model-building. We put the right people in who related to people so they could draw out consumer needs. We mixed it up with different approaches, different thought styles, and that little team generated over 20 unique packaging innovations in just a few months...a lot of those didn't get developed and put into the market until much, much later."

Those lessons also provided the core values for Rigaud's post-P&G life, in the Enova automotive supplier companies he founded after seeing the doors of the NURFC open. Enova's acronym, RIDE— Responsiveness, Integrity, Diversity, and Excellence—"comes right out of P&G training." Owning the largest tire and wheel assembler in the country in the past few years has been "all about discipline," Rigaud says—putting the components together according to specs and delivering "just in time and in-sequence, properly inflated with tire pressure monitors, with uniformity testing completed, high quality, so they hit the road and give the ultimate consumer the best 'RIDE.'" He says, "We're customer intimate, so we know what the customer wants and we deliver it, and that's all Procter philosophy."

Enova has joined with Nehemiah Manufacturing, which has built a plant in a depressed part of Cincinnati, a job-creation mission fueled by Rigaud's years leading the Freedom Center project. While heading that project, Rigaud developed an understanding of freedom based on Abraham Maslow's famous hierarchy of need, rising from the physiological up through safety, love, and belonging, and then to esteem and self-actualization. Rigaud's freedom pyramid rests on freedom from—discrimination, oppression, pain and suffering—then rising through freedom of—self-expression and basic human rights— to freedom to—actualization and empowerment. "So the thing I'm devoting the rest of my life to is, how do you take people from where they are, either literally where they are, or where they perceive themselves to be, and help move them to higher and higher levels of freedom?" he says. "How do you give them the wherewithal to do that, giving them the inspiration and the challenge to do that, and the tools to do that, and so having a successful consumer business or manufacturing business and giving folks a chance to work and become ultimately empowered?"

Rigaud credits the mentoring he got at P&G with anchoring his core values and principles. And no one played a more important part in that process than his Section Head, Paul Bates, who welcomed

Rigaud and his new wife, just hours after they had gotten married, at the Cincinnati airport. With two days before the new hire was due to report at the office, Bates took the newlyweds on a tour of their new home city before delivering them to their honeymoon hotel. He "basically became my mentor, my best friend, and best friend of the family," Rigaud recalls. "He was remarkable. He tailor-made a training program for me, written in a big booklet that I followed religiously. He had written up every step, every experiment, and every product test he asked me to do and I reported on those religiously. Yet, he was a really gentle man who coached me and coaxed me along until I got over my naivety. He was excellent."

Rigaud remembers "at least three more people like that in my career, spaced out typically at the right time." One of them was Ken Ericson, who gave Rigaud his first promotion. Another was Mike Milligan, who championed Rigaud's move from research and development to marketing and general management, at a time when such moves were rare. "It was Mike who said, 'Ed, you can do anything you want in this company, and I'll see to it.' He did. And he was also a guy who, when I lost my spleen in an automobile accident (in 1983), sat in the hospital for 11 straight days, who came from work and held my wife's hand through two surgeries while I was dying. That's the Procter I knew."

Such actions made a deep impression, in turn inspiring Rigaud to want to model values for others. When he was appointed Director of Product Development in the food service and lodging products division, he found a group "not very trusting or welcoming. I don't know what the context was for them before I arrived, but for whatever reason, they were very, very withdrawn and cautious." Rigaud scheduled one-on-one interviews with everyone in the group over the next few weeks and then organized a picnic-cum-business meeting. He introduced the team to HOFF, "a way to express my values and principles: Honesty, Openness, Fairness, and Fun. Actually, the last F was 'fulfillment,' but I said it as 'fun' to make it simple. Then I talked to them about these principles and how I really believed in them and over time, they really did take onto this. In fact, I run into some of those folks out of that organization periodically, and they always bring up HOFF and how they took on HOFF as a way to describe their values. And in subsequent outings we had, they created T-shirts. There was one that had a dragon on it, and it was called 'HOFF the Magic Dragon.'"

Rigaud's P&G years also exposed him to the Ned Herrmann Brain Dominance Instrument, developed to identify people's ways of thinking and processing information—analytical, sequential, interpersonal, or imaginative. "I just absorbed it and put into my daily life, and I still use it today in my company. In terms of how my brain operates, it is much more intellectual than it is social/emotional, though I've learned to develop some of my social/emotional skills as well. But analysis and synthesis, those two are what I live on. I love creativity. I love building, I love innovation. So, the analysis part that I learned so well at P&G, I probably would not have learned otherwise, because I lean much more toward synthesis. But I know how to do analysis, and I got disciplined into doing it at Procter. You know, the one-pagers make you do it. Every aspect of P&G makes you very strong analytically."

Rigaud had been attracted to P&G in the first place by its reputation for excellence. Though he had an appreciation for art and music, he had graduated with a chemistry degree from Xavier University of Louisiana, anticipating a career in research and development. "But then they took me in the chemistry labs and did a half day of interviews there before realizing that this wasn't what I was interested in, and the guy said, 'Maybe you're a products' researcher?' and I said, 'What's that?' He started talking about how they understood consumer needs and turned those into product concepts and ultimately products in the marketplace that had your personal creativity in them, and I said, 'You just hit it perfectly. That's what I want to do. I've never heard of this, but that's what I want to do.'"

"So, over the years I learned about visioning and team building and innovation; innovation's a huge one for me—innovative thinking. And I learned about leadership and collaboration, and so all those things fit my personality and my value system very well." Looking back on over 35 years in business with P&G and honored contributions to civic and community initiatives, Rigaud has far more hits than misses to speak about, but he is not afraid to address the strikeouts. While he knows that it does not pay to dwell on them, he believes it is important to face failures squarely and learn from them before moving on. He says that it is often in the downturns that the principles and foundations that will assure success are forged and firmed. "You learn from failures, and P&G lets you fail," he says. "The failure was never one person's, and that was part of the collaborative approach. There was never just one person who screwed it up."

Rigaud recalls the Cold Snap mess of the late 1970s. The idea was a new kind of frozen dessert that could be made at home. Test products created from real ice cream and fresh ingredients were great, but the planned rollout versions were "made from this chemical sludge—slurry that took forever to freeze and tasted like a chemistry set." A junior member of the Cold Snap team, Rigaud also remembers other challenges he witnessed at P&G: Pringles—testing well but poorly produced when it first came to the market, slowing its early acceptance—and the decision to scrap Rely tampons because of concerns over toxic shock syndrome, even though a definite link was not proven. "There was weeping and gnashing over what to do, over should we scrap it or not?" Rigaud remembers. "Or should we just try to push it through? Procter always tends to make the right and courageous decision even if there's some gnashing of teeth, and they do the right thing. That's integrity!"

Originally invited to take on leadership of the NUFRC project when he was Vice President of Food and Beverage Products, Rigaud became an executive on loan for two years, but he felt from the start it would require more time. He told friend Bob Wehling, to whom he reported progress, "the average for a new museum of this magnitude is nine years." Rigaud's stay at the NUFRC was extended, during which time he recruited John Pepper right after his first retirement from P&G. The two of them plus a team of staff and volunteers raised more than $100 million for the project. Then, as Rigaud entered his sixth year at the NUFRC, Wehling told him "you have either got to come back, or you have got to retire," Rigaud recalled. "And I said, 'I don't want to come back. I've tasted what this is about and what I can do on my own now. I'm not going to go to work for somebody. I'm going to go build something well,' and I knew I could do it. My confidence had been built over those years to the point where there wasn't anything I didn't think I could do or accomplish, and I think the breakthrough with the creation of the Freedom Pyramid helped me to decide where I wanted to put that effort and that energy, and it's still driving me. My life's mission now is to light that same fire in as many young people as I can touch!"

11

Jill Beraud

Family baking and fancy bras may seem to be worlds apart when it comes to branding, but they share a core touch point that links the kitchen and the closet that captures the essence of Jill Beraud's marketing gift. Both markets "have a lot of emotional content," says the Chief Marketing Officer and President, Joint Ventures, PepsiCo Beverages Americas. "You just have to understand where to look for it." Beraud speaks from her experience of working with Procter & Gamble's (P&G's) Duncan Hines cake and cookie line in her formative years at the company, and then transferring the principles she learned there to Victoria's Secret underwear for Limited Brands. "There is very high emotional content in baking mixes," Beraud says, recalling the importance of "really understanding the role of the brand and the product to a mom, and the fact that baking for a family and the children is an expression of love and caring."

Beraud joined P&G's food and beverage division right out of business school and helped turn around declining Duncan Hines cake mix sales. She was appointed Crisco Oil Brand Manager of Duncan Hines Specialty Mixes before taking on responsibility for all baking mix products. "When I went to focus groups and heard women talk about the experience of baking and eating Duncan Hines, she says, "There was a lot of passion and loyalty around chocolate."

Fast-forward to Beraud's time as Chief Marketing Officer for Victoria's Secret, and she found a similar strong sense of identity with the brand. "There was a high level of passion. When consumers would walk into a Victoria's Secret store, they described it as a transformative experience," she says. "With the music, the silk, the scents, it was a very multisensory experience. Many women would say that they would go into a Victoria's Secret store just to relax, if they just needed a break in the day."

Looking back, Beraud sees that she was able to take some of the "tremendous fundamentals" she learned in consumer marketing and brand-building principles at P&G and translate them for specialty retailing in the fashion and beauty business, an export that surprised many. "I treasured every day that I was there," Beraud says of her 1986 to 1991 P&G career. "It was one of the best experiences of my life." In her P&G days, she was tutored in "the best marketing fundamentals anywhere in the world, in terms of understanding the consumer, understanding business principles, and really taking those lessons to figure out how to drive strategic business growth and brand growth." She appreciates the training she received. "Nobody is better than P&G at training and developing leaders. They really taught us the discipline of how to think through an opportunity and come to a conclusion that made sense to build a business." Additionally, she was taught that "to be a really successful leader, you have to know how to develop talent—and nobody does that better than P&G. Having my roots at P&G, I've taken that with me throughout my career, and it has really enabled me to lead large groups of people through change and through enormous growth."

In the years since leaving P&G—which included time with an international management consulting firm and a season running her own New York City advertising agency—Beraud has, like everyone, had to expand her understanding of effective branding to embrace the increasingly multifaceted nature of business. "It's not just retail; it's 360-degree, multichannel storytelling," she notes. "As well as bricks and mortar, there is e-commerce and catalogs...multichannel, global brands. Building brands is really about storytelling and being able to tell the story of a brand through multiple touch points...All the interactions between the consumer and the product [are] really what [separate] successful brands from those that are not."

Just as superior cooking requires a certain flair in addition to the basic ingredients, so "there is an art and science to managing brands," Beraud says. She anchors that observation in her P&G experience working on Duncan Hines, when her team went beyond the time-honored commitment to learning what people want through focus groups to try to learn more about their consumers. "It was critical to gaining insight into how consumers thought about the product, the brand, and the whole experience of interacting with the brand," she says. "So we would cook and bake with people—we would go into their kitchens. It was a real learning experience. It helped us understand how to innovate, it helped us understand how to communicate better and really tap into that emotional connectivity. But, it wasn't just a science; it was an art and a science."

Another skill Beraud became grounded in while at P&G was being able to "lead change while managing continuity—because that's actually how you win. It's not about just managing change," she says, "because that means you are always one step behind, responding to what the consumer wants. And that way, you're not going to be the first to market." Rather, "it's actually leading change. That's how you become a leader in the category. It's about having foresight and anticipating change, as opposed to reacting to it."

She was asked to help build Crisco Corn Oil's market share. Although "very few people were talking about growth of the Hispanic market" at that time, Beraud saw an opportunity there. She created the first Hispanic cooking show, *La Cocina de Crisco*, aired five days a week on Spanish-language networks. Bear in mind that Crisco was competing with Mazola Oil, which enjoyed major loyalty with Hispanic consumers because of its history as the established market leader in South America. *La Cocina de Crisco* targeted Mom. "She was still doing all of the cooking in the house and, just like any mother, she was looking for meal solutions, and fun and variety and pleasing her family every day, because cooking—just like baking—is a way of expressing your love and taking care of your family. And we were giving her solutions and entertaining her every day." That successful move—tripling business in a year—was all about anticipating change rather than managing it, Beraud says: "Just identifying that the Hispanic cohort was going to be an important one and that you needed to speak to them in a different way and target them in a different culture."

The Crisco experience also underscores a principle Beraud discovered at P&G—one she has emphasized in her career since. It is that trust, which some say is the essence of connecting with consumers, is not so much the end point as the beginning. "Trust is a critical thing, but you need so much more than trust; you need brand differentiation to really drive consumer loyalty," Beraud says. Trust is just "the entry point, the price of entry. Trust is the foundation. But trust is not going to differentiate your product from another. There's so much hyper competition out there—you have to do way more than offer trust. To really build a brand and an emotional connection, you have to surprise and delight, and capture the consumers' imaginations and/or solve a problem."

Beraud carries that conviction into her current role with PepsiCo, overseeing all its beverages. "It's about putting the consumer and the consumer needs and consumer lifestyles first," she says. "Not just understanding her or him today, but where they're headed, because if you can really understand their lifestyle and what's missing, you can help innovate, to meet not just their needs today, but their needs tomorrow." Not that it's easy. "Everything is at hyper speed now. Cycle times have been shortened. People's attention spans are more fragmented. It's much more challenging than it was."

12

Jane J. Thompson

What is the difference between managing a household product brand and overseeing an innovative financial services program that impacts millions of Americans? About thirty years and a lot of practice. The scope of Jane J. Thompson's responsibilities has changed dramatically, from her early business career of leading the development of Mr. Clean, to when she headed Walmart's new bank-alternative money centers. But the fundamentals remained the same.

"My first job at Procter strongly shaped how I think about business," she says. "The general management philosophy that I learned as a Brand Manager influences the way I designed product management inside Walmart's financial services." In her four foundational years at Procter & Gamble (P&G), Thompson was given immediate responsibility to drive her assigned brand, supported by a group that helped managed the P&L. That same level of empowerment and trust was extended to her Walmart team working in financial services. It is a business approach that simply works. "There is a Product Manager for Walmart MoneyCard, another for check cashing. They have a profit and loss statement with marketing budgets," Thompson says. "I was lucky to start in a job where I was taught general management skills from the beginning. All through my career, I have always taken the view of the General Manager." At the heart of it, that means believing in your product and the benefits it provides consumers, she believes. "Part of it comes from just who I am, but I am sure it was strengthened at P&G: We thought what we were doing was really important. We believed that the differences in our bar soap versus another were very distinctive to our consumers. We believed our products made a difference in their lives."

That same sense of purpose fueled Thompson's leadership of Walmart's financial services expansion, bringing many money services to the estimated 60 million-plus Americans who are underserved by existing bank services. "I feel very good about helping customers save money. I'm cashing payroll checks for $3; they go to a cash advance location and might pay $9, $12, $15, or more to cash that check. I love that I saved them money and helped them live better. That certainly is what drove us at Walmart. Likewise, P&G Brand Managers feel strongly about the brand that they're in charge of, and that motivates them."

That sense of mission is strengthened, she feels, by the immediate ownership instilled to P&G employees from day one. "You had a sense that the product belonged to you, that it was yours to grow and protect. I felt that protective nature with our Walmart financial services." Not that fostering a sense of ownership needs to mean giving people complete freedom to do whatever they want. Thompson remembers as a relative P&G newcomer making a pitch to change Camay soap's packaging. Camay's wrapper was designed like the Zest wrapper with an inner cardboard enclosure, but Camay didn't open very easily. The Zest wrapper was more paper, whereas Camay's wrapper, to be more feminine, was made of a pearlescent oil-based derivative that didn't tear like paper. Thompson says that the Camay package opened with ease by pinching any corner and pulling the end of the wrapper; it zipped right off. Thompson did her homework, presenting a recommendation that Camay go from its knapsack wrap to new packaging—one that would not only work better, but save money because it did not require the inner cardboard enclosure. She made her case, solo as she recalls, to then-Advertising Manager John Pepper. "I showed him the consumer research and presented a recommendation including the cost savings. He decided it was too risky," she recalls—confident to this day that she was right. "I still think, 'I could have saved money, the product would have worked better, and the customers would have liked it better.' I don't know why he didn't like my recommendation, but he was very conservative about it. That was before the price of oil began rising. I think today he would have agreed, especially since the savings would be even greater."

What stands out for Thompson is not so much the rejection as the affirmation. "I'm a Brand Assistant at that time; I'm not a Brand Manager yet, and they let me go in and make this pitch, in my own words. That's such a confidence booster. Even though he said no, he certainly listened."

P&G's success in developing leaders, she reflects, is in the "ecosystem culture." Starting with the eighth-floor executives personally interacting with the Brand teams through the famous one-page memos, the ecosystem was built on trust, checks and balances, and innovation. It was also built on a level of commitment to the development of people that they expected to lead thinking and initiatives from early in their careers. "We didn't use the word 'matrix' in those days, but you always knew in the end the Ad Manager could call you in and want to look at your advertising. And the Sales Manager could nix your promotion idea. It was a high-performance, team environment with a lot of energy and drive." At the heart of her P&G learning was that everything starts with the customer and his or her needs. "The focus was on market research and translating consumer needs back to a P&L, ultimately to build shareholder value."

Thompson embraced P&G's long-term view of business, a core value of choosing sometimes to go slower to be sure of going further. A case in point: In developing Walmart's MoneyCard program, an individual on Thompson's team argued for putting a competitive prepaid debit card on the store shelves alongside Walmart's MoneyCard because it would bring in extra money short term. "I said, 'I don't care about the money short term; I care about the brand long term. If we're not building our brand, the Walmart MoneyCard, then I don't think we're winning the game.' Interestingly, a lot of very smart people didn't get the point. I may make more for the moment, more money with this competitive card in that shelf space since it is higher priced, but it is taking share from my Walmart brand. What a revelation."

As one of the first wave of up-and-coming women in corporate leadership, joining P&G straight out of undergraduate school, Thompson feels that "every one of my P&G bosses [was] very supportive, given that I was one of the first women there and also an undergraduate. I got promoted in the same order as the MBAs, and I thought I was always treated very well, with great respect." Leaving P&G for MBA studies at Harvard, progressing through senior positions with McKinsey & Company and Sears before joining Walmart in 2002, Thompson admits, "I don't know how many dozens of times I have gone back to how the P&G brand structure works. It's all about finding the customer need, figuring out how to deliver it and how to market it.

"P&G operating values were so embedded in those short four years. While I was a President and had a very big P&L, I still approached the business a lot like I did as a Brand Manager." Thompson continued to hold to P&G's commitment to listening to the customer. "I still went to focus groups. I sat there behind the glass. If somebody was doing focus groups, I didn't want to hear it second- or thirdhand. I want to hear the customers talking, because you hear their pain points; you hear their passion. You know when they talk on and on that something's really clicking. You can't get it later from videotapes, and you certainly can't get it from a written report."

To Jane Thompson, being customer-centered is everybody's business. This means building products that can open easily all the way to banking services that deliver savings for families trying to stay within a budget. In a nutshell, building a process that centers on customers and the value of the experience is a top priority. The key elements of that process are being driven to truly understand customer needs, making sure your product or service emotionally answers that need, wisely designing your products or delivery of services, and having the vigilance to keep looking ahead to the next customer need. "I actually think business can be that simple." Simple maybe, but certainly not easy!

13

Robert A. Miller

Few people have seen the inner workings of as many different markets as Robert A. Miller. From beer and betting to mail and mascara, he has witnessed the unique challenges of firms in different industries—and he has concluded that there is a singular success factor common to each. "From a performance standpoint, I have seen that the companies who walk the talk with regard to integrity perform at a much higher level than those companies that do not." The thing that mattered most to him throughout his career is the whole issue of integrity. This truth he finds rooted in the foundations laid for him in his four years with Procter & Gamble (P&G) after he graduated from business school, a period that prepared him for an adventurous career that has taken him from coast to coast and from established brands to feisty start-ups. "The one thing that I attribute to my success over time has been the belief system that was given to me at P&G," he says. "I was blessed to start out at a place like P&G, because I learned what truly mattered, early. I didn't learn it late. I learned it from the beginning. And, I always believed that what I was taught at P&G was right!"

For Miller, the early learning about integrity was followed quickly by two other vital core values: leadership and ownership. "They say that if you have integrity, nothing else matters, and if you don't have integrity, nothing else matters," he says. "Well, at Procter & Gamble, being intellectually honest and being fact-based and nonpolitical, operating within the letter and the spirit of the law, acting like an owner—all those things formed a great foundation for me going forward." From his very first contact with P&G, beginning in an interview with Puffs Brand Manager Bob Baker, "I first learned the importance of always trying to do the right thing and being honest and direct." He and Baker hit it off. Miller recalls, "How the company interacted with me from that point forward was very crisp, very honest, and very deliberate." Miller quickly came to appreciate the importance of leadership, too. "The leadership orientation displayed by the people of P&G impressed me from the very outset—having that strong desire to be the best, to lead in our markets, to get there before our competitors. Having a clear vision about what it is that we're doing is something that has served me in my time since then—being strategically oriented, believing that you have a God-given right to be number one in your markets."

That sense of focus also demands personal accountability, Miller says. "In a brand organization, you're taught that you're running a large company here and you are accountable for the promises you make to the company, in terms of volume, sales, and revenue, and that you are accountable for the management of the precious assets associated with that." In his four years with P&G, Miller covered a lot of ground and many markets. Before leaving as an Assistant Brand Manager in 1983, he worked in toilet goods, personal care products, surgical products, and patient care. His responsibilities included Secret deodorant, Abound hair conditioner, and Attends adult diapers. Through those varied assignments, he was consistently "taught to act like an owner, and that's something that never leaves you." Miller took that mind-set with him to positions with FedEx, Anheuser Busch, Maybelline, Harrah's Entertainment, and General Motors, among others, before founding his own consultancy. A stint with the digital mapper Tele Atlas gave him an inside view of doing business in a non-U.S. owned operation. From his travels, Miller notes the strength of "companies with truly strong belief systems, truly strong cultures driven by the basics like integrity, ownership, talent, trust, and a passion for winning—those companies," he says, "seem to do very, very well over time."

Although new businesses have often turned to former P&Gers for an infusion of some of the company's admired DNA, "I have seen that sometimes in the excitement and stress and competitive environment of start-ups, when push comes to shove, the interest in things like integrity seems to not be as strong as you'd like," he says. "It's kind of hard if you don't have a window into how important or how powerful a belief system is." Miller contrasts the difference in the ways some start-ups and P&G view one of their key assets—their talent. "Sometimes start-ups are unable to get the right people hired because time is of the essence—there's a short window in terms of getting the product ready for market, getting it launched, and at the same time, getting the requisite investments to continue to come into the company. I've been in start-ups that hired people and then decided later on whether or not they fit. That is, if they have a critical need for someone to write code, or someone to do design work, or whatever, they get who they could get, and then they figure it out later." That is markedly different from the care P&G takes in talent selection. Miller says of P&G, "It was such a powerful place in which to learn that I can say it is the only place that I have ever been where I could truly say that the person above me knew more than me—always," because of P&G's commitment to choosing the right people and developing them over time.

Miller has made a point of replicating P&G's people focus, seeing many of those who have worked for him go on to greater heights as marketing officers or company owners. "Mostly that's because they were smart people to start with—very eager to grow and develop," he says. But "I spent an extraordinary amount of personal development time with my team members, too, to help them get to where they wanted to go—and it's all because that's what happened to me."

Miller saw a similar commitment to its people by FedEx. "One of the things that attracted me to FedEx was the company's belief system, which was focused on its people and its customers. The company's People, Service, Profit philosophy was reflective of the P&G

way. FedEx believes that if it takes care of its people (in all the ways that you should take care of people)—development, training, paying them properly, benefits—they will in turn deliver a superior service, which will thus enable the company to meet its product objectives." Failing to make this investment doesn't only harm those who get chewed up and tossed aside. It simply makes the job of building a business "much, much harder than it should be," Miller says. "If you would simply take the time to do it right, you'd be much better off." Having said that, some upstart businesses see great success without those kind of moorings—at least, in the short run. "What they don't know is that 10 years out, 20 years out is the real story, and that if you have built a foundation that doesn't include integrity, the leadership orientation, the ownership orientation, trust, then you probably built your business on a shaky footing."

Miller believes that "the extent to which a company early on invests in certain bedrock principles, certain bedrock beliefs, it will serve them well over time. It's just such a powerful thing when an organization can say, 'These are the things we believe in,' and that's what Procter & Gamble did. They put it up for everyone to see. It was how the company believed in developing and moving its people and its business forward, its commitment to knowing more about its customers and their needs, knowing more about how to deliver a better product, knowing more about how to persuasively communicate what its products offered that make a difference versus its competition. In general, the company just knew more, because, as a part of its belief system, it invested in knowing more because it believed that that was the way to win."

Offering advice from his vantage point to bullish new businesses on how to activate a beginning belief system, Miller says that "If you are going to start someplace, start with integrity." He looks back on his first of two tours of duty with FedEx, after leaving P&G. "What I observed right off the bat at FedEx is that they had populated themselves with a group of like-minded Senior Executives, who all had in common one thing, and that was integrity," he recalls. One of the favorite expressions inside the company was "Seek Truth." He says, "They all tried to do the right thing, be fact-based, nonpolitical, honest, and straightforward. It's like when Google first started and they had a motto that they started with 'Do no evil.' They had that motto in part because some start-ups were doing evil. I mean, they were not operating within the letter or the spirit of the law. They were doing some things from a privacy standpoint, for example, that you shouldn't. And Google said, 'We're not going to be like that. We're going to do no evil.'" If integrity is fundamental, then next is "populate yourself with people who have strong customer advocacy orientation, leadership orientation, or a passion for winning. Whatever it is that makes sense in the context of your business and the market in which you compete, you should do that and make it not just a sometimes thing, but an all-the-time thing. Your key decisions should be driven in part by a beginning set of beliefs from which you are seeking to grow your business."

Core values and a belief system are timeless and can help you win more versus your competition. "Core values become strategic, and over time they differentiate you in the marketplace. FedEx delivers 'absolutely, positively' because their people refuse to have it any other way; it's central to the character of the company," he says. "They are keeping a promise. This is the lesson of P&G. Core values are about keeping promises. Integrity is keeping promises to each other, your customers, your stockholders, and the communities of which you are a part. Leadership is about staying true to your objectives and your stewardship. And, accountability and ownership are keeping promises of personal accountability and the ownership mentality as a key part of how you should operate when responsible for a business."

Part III
Core Values and Teamwork

14

Dave Brandon

If anyone knows that effective organizations share the same essentials—no matter how varied and distinct their particular area of focus might be from others—it's Dave Brandon. His 35-plus-year career ranged from consumer goods through marketing services to the food industry and eventually came full circle to his alma mater. Now Director of Intercollegiate Athletics at University of Michigan— where on a football scholarship he originally intended to pursue a career as a teacher and coach—Brandon is also uniquely qualified to talk about how to understand and strengthen organizational cultures. He credits much of that to his unplanned first job: five years with Procter & Gamble (P&G), where he served as a Sales Representative, District Field Rep, and Unit Manager in Food Products. Although he had a job lined up as varsity team coach, when he was contacted by a P&G recruiter on campus who heard about him, Brandon decided to give the business world a shot.

"I was a classic example of P&G's willingness to hire talent as opposed to resumes or pedigrees," Brandon says. "I had never had a business course in my life...I tell people I was fortunate enough to get my MBA at the school of Procter & Gamble, because they were willing to hire me as someone who they thought had potential and who had fundamental basic qualities that they felt that they could utilize, teaching me what I needed to know to be successful."

It was a thorough if informal course: how to hire people, recruit and assess talent, give performance reviews, develop programs for developing people, plan successions, market, manage a brand, and interact with customers. Those were all concepts that I needed to learn, because I didn't have the benefit of any of that teaching during my college experience," Brandon says. "Not all companies are willing to take that risk. Not that many companies are necessarily ambitious enough to find and develop talent in that way, and so for that, I will be eternally grateful to P&G."

Among the other lessons while at P&G, Brandon learned commitment to excellence that impacts not only those outside the organization—its customers—but those within. "I always refer to P&G as a first-class company," he says, "a company that cares about how it treats its people and is classy in its approach. It was a company that always cared about how we looked and presented ourselves."

One of the chief core values that Brandon took away from P&G was the commitment to do the right thing the right way. "The whole issue of integrity, having that moral compass, was incredibly helpful to me in my formative years, working for a company where integrity was everything. It was not just some slogan on the wall." There were situations, as a young manager, where it would have been easy to bend things a little to ensure a favorable outcome. But "we just didn't do that stuff. I was taught that you play by the rules. You shoot it straight down the middle. You communicate to your customers exactly the truth, whether they like it or not."

His next move, to marketing company Valassis Communications—where in his 20 years, he helped take the business public and became CEO—placed him "out there in the wild, wild west during the junk bond days. With all the things that were going on, that moral compass was something that was exceedingly important."

Brandon refers to his time under famed University of Michigan football coach Bob Schembechler to frame another P&G essential he caught while with the company: "It's all about the fundamentals of basic blocking and tackling. We live in a world where people often want to create complexity because it makes smart people feel smarter. But at the end of the day, P&G had this wonderful way of taking complex problems and coming up with simple, direct solutions... Their approach was, 'Here are the basic things you need to do well.'"

Brandon surprised many people with another unlikely turn, when in 1999 he left Valassis to become CEO at Domino's in the wake of the pizza chain founder Tom Monaghan's departure. In the decade he spent there, before returning to UM in 2010, Brandon oversaw the business's growth to more than 9,000 stores in 67 countries. As the self-acknowledged "poster child for moving from one completely diverse industry and leadership role to another," Brandon has some advice for leaders making big transitions. In the first few months, just "shut up and listen and learn. Don't go into the job feeling like you have to be the answer man and impress everybody with how bright and experienced you are." Brandon does the opposite. "I get to know my teams. I get to find out where the weaknesses and strengths are. I use the advantage of having a fresh set of eyes as an opportunity to ask any question."

Brandon says he has become famous for telling folks, "'I'm new around here'—and getting away with that as long as I can. It affords the ability to probe in and ask questions and really delve into the business at a level that helps you understand the mechanics of what makes the business work." He advises, "Have the confidence to not feel like you have got to come to work every day and prove yourself. Over time, there'll be plenty of opportunity to gain the credibility that you need as a leader and to exercise your prerogative as a leader, but in the initial stages, listen and learn and be open and absorb and formulate your plan."

Incoming leaders have typically been tasked to bring about change, but you can't change an organization "until you understand the culture, and you can't understand the culture until you spend some time with it, get a feel for what it is and how it evolved, what areas are going to be easy to change, and which areas are going to be more difficult." Tradition is often woven deep into an organization's culture—especially when you are dealing with time-honored institutions like UM, with its 130-plus years, the winningest program in the history of college football, with at least one team captain who went on to become President of the United States. The trick is to determine which elements of tradition are foundations for the future and which are fault lines of the past. Some, like UM's rich sports heritage, "really drive the excitement and energy around Michigan Athletics and are things that we can market and use to create the positive energy we need to be successful" again. These kind of past assets are "the pillars on which the culture stands and the thing that motivates and is a source of pride to not only your current employees, but your prospective employees." But former glories can sometimes be a crutch, Brandon says. "'This is the way we've always done things'—so everything becomes a tradition, and consequently we don't change and we don't innovate."

He said of his first year at UM, "one of the real balancing acts I've had is making those decisions around...those traditions that are really important, that we really value, that are truly a positive influence on the culture and the future of the enterprise, versus when traditions are being used to cover up the fact that we really don't want to change or we really don't want to step up to a new world and a new way of doing things." Although Brandon recognizes the new vision a pair of outside eyes can bring to an enterprise, he also believes in leveraging as much internal strength as possible. It's an emphasis he has kept from his time with P&G, where he saw a commitment to finding raw new talent and then nurturing it. "Every place I've gone, I've implemented college recruiting, development plans where you identify developmental employees, succession planning around developmental employees, special training programs for developmental employees...that was the P&G recipe. Now we're in a world where, often, it is so comfortable and easy to just go out and find the headhunter who's going to bring to you the list of candidates. It's a bit of laziness. In the short term, maybe it's a little bit easier to just go grab somebody who's been there, done that, as opposed to reaching into your organization and identifying that individual who's really looking for his or her chance."

Brandon is proud that in his 22 years as a CEO, every Chief Financial Officer, Chief Marketing Officer, and Chief Information Officer he has appointed has been a promotion, "meaning in all of those key positions, I have never gone out and recruited someone that was doing a job someplace else and brought him in to do it for me. I truly believe you should never underestimate the power of someone who has something to prove. I want that individual who has been waiting on the bench for that time for the coach to tap him or her on the shoulder and say, 'Now it's your turn to go in and win the game.' I think the energy and the sense of urgency that people bring to that first opportunity they have to really show what they can do and what they're prepared for is powerful. Procter did that with the promote-from-within mentality. When I was at Procter, it was unheard of for them to acquire a company, bring in a bunch of new people, put them into key roles, or even go out and hire somebody at a senior level; it just didn't happen."

Looking for people within to help take an organization to the next level presupposes another essential, though—that you have the right people there in the first place to draw on. While Brandon is reluctant to look for outside expertise, he knows that finding the skills and talent needed within means developing a reservoir of talent—requires recruiting the right people for the future. "It all starts with who you hire, and who you hire is a by-product of how you hire," he says, reflecting on his introduction to P&G. "They didn't wait for me to come sign up, because had they done that, it would have never happened: I didn't even know where the business school's placement office was. Recruiters came to campus and they prerecruited...they dug around this campus and interviewed leaders on campus to find people with talent and attitude and energy. I think we live in a world where far too many organizations take the safe way out. If you've got your MBA and you went to a big-time school, then de facto, you're talent. I don't necessarily believe that. It certainly hasn't been my experience. I'm a big believer in using the proper practices with your hiring and recruiting—ones that set the tone for the kind of strengths you're going to have in your organization. I have practiced that in virtually every leadership job I've had, and I've been very fortunate to be a part of organizations that have created billions of dollars of shareholder value while creating cultures that are recognized nationally for being highly successful and great places to work. I don't know how it gets any better than that."

Though he has been successful as the leader of two New York Stock Exchange companies, rather than point to the balance sheets, Brandon is as apt to cite inclusion in the list of 100 best companies to work for, three years in a row, as a favorable metric. "The strength of your enterprise is in the talent that you recruit and the way you treat that talent. To me, your leadership style has to lead to a superior workplace environment," he says. "We want people who work at our organization to go home and over dinner say, 'You can't believe what happened at work today. At two o'clock they brought in a bunch of ice cream trucks and gave us all ice cream'...coming up with special ways to make that culture unique and make that workplace experience something special that people want to talk about. It's not all about your business model, financial wizardry, or outsmarting the competitors with your fancy footwork. If you don't pay attention to those people who come to work every day—who have a lot of discretionary time and attention they can either give to you or give to somebody else—you're just not going to achieve the success that you have the potential to achieve. To me, it's all about the people, the strength of your middle management, the ability that you have to connect with your frontline workers in every way." It all goes back, he says, to what he observed at P&G. "The way they got things done: They never did it around or through people—they did it *with* people. That's why I have such great respect for the company and, hell, I'm still talking about them like I love them, and I haven't worked there for 30 years."

15

Brad Casper

Like high-wire walkers, transformational leaders must be able to balance two sides to successfully navigate the thin line across a chasm of change. They need to be enough of an outsider to see things in a new way, and enough of an insider to know how to communicate those insights effectively to people potentially threatened by change. Brad Casper, a Procter & Gamble (P&G) employee from 1985–2001, mastered this navigational art in his nine years leading some of P&G's noted expansion in Asia. There he developed the nature of what he calls being a "cultural chameleon," characterized by an ability to blend in and practice situational leadership in new situations and new cultures. That Casper thrived so long in a region that had previously been a career graveyard for so many American executives—mangled in a collision of West-East cultures, where more managers "left in body bags than succeeded"—speaks of the rare skills he developed.

But international success didn't come easily or automatically. Tapped for an international Brand Manager's assignment after just three years with the company, Casper headed for Kobe, Japan in 1989 with his wife on what they assumed would be a two-year assignment. They arrived with minimal knowledge of the language and limited cross-cultural preparation. The challenge was not just to learn how to mesh general Western values with his new Eastern context, but to discover how to integrate some foundational P&G orientations that did not fit with Japanese tradition. For example, "being vocal, speaking out, and having your points of view heard ran contrary to a culture where unspoken language is as important as the spoken word," he says. "I came over, like a lot of Americans, with a brand of leadership that was to speak first and listen second. I learned that the opposite was often true in Japan. You really had to do a good job of listening—in some cases, even bite your tongue and sit in a meeting quietly, listening, sympathizing and digesting all the verbal and nonverbal language and being one of the last to speak. There is a Japanese proverb to the effect that 'the one who speaks the least may actually be the wisest.' As such, Japanese revere listening and are encouraged to practice 'enthusiastic listening,' evidenced by vigorous nodding and short verbal affirmations. This communication philosophy transformed my management and leadership style—not only with P&G but after I left the company."

Although he grew up in the shadows of P&G's Cincinnati headquarters in a prominent suburb where many P&G executives lived, he did not arrive at the company straight from a university as do so many. He returned to the city with General Electric, with whom he had taken a job as a financial analyst upon graduating from Virginia Tech. A conversation with a P&G executive at the wedding of a mutual friend sparked Casper's interest in his hometown business, "and when I got the brand management brochure, I was convinced that this is what I wanted to do for my career."

Casper's adaptation in Asia actually flowed from holding to one of P&G's foundational values: its belief that its people were its most important asset. He demonstrated that in ways that his Japanese teams could understand, showing respect for their culture. He witnessed enough "unsuccessful behavior" from Americans to know that "temper, impatience, disrespect, and cutting people down" did not work. Instead, he learned to foster "nemawashi"—drawing people together around an idea. "The Japanese must process concepts as a group. It's a group culture rather than an individual culture, coalescing around an idea. I saw how critical it was to getting collaboration—some would argue consensus. The Japanese culture is about harmony, not disharmony." At the same time, Casper knew he had to be careful to match the needs of the people he was leading with those of the people to whom he was reporting. Coming from a North American-centric company, he needed to find a happy balance of style that blended the best of the Western trained management with the values cherished by the East. He says, "You had to hybrid yourself with vision, values, and leadership."

Casper stood out in Asia—becoming General Manager in Hong Kong and China after his time in Japan—and not just for his cultural sensitivity. At 6 feet 5 inches, he also towered above most people around him—but found that being something of an oddity was also an asset. He found that in moving to Asia, he became a minority for the first time, and this helped him build self-awareness and ultimately empathy in ways he doesn't think he would have developed had he remained in Cincinnati. Charged in 1990 with helping launch P&G's recently acquired Pantene shampoo in the Far East, Casper mulled over this challenge as he commuted daily on Japan's trains and subways to and from work. "I was nearly a foot taller than almost everyone around, and the crowded trains afforded me one incredible view of the tops of everybody's head," he says. The healthiest hair, he observed, was also the shiniest. "You could literally see the sun coming in through a train window and forming this crown of light or halo around the top of someone's head." That insight prompted consumer research confirming that shiny hair was viewed as the healthiest. "We then rolled out that test into almost every other country in the Far East and, without exception, we found that was a universal truth." The positioning of Pantene was born. Casper's commute-time insight became the positioning thrust for Pantene's rollout globally—one that led to the product to become one of the most successful new hair care launches ever, and one of P&G's biggest successes. "We didn't create a commercial; we made a healthy, shiny hair video, and it became the idea, the visual background that brought the entire brand to life, not just in Japan, but around the world. It was really the Olympics of hair in motion!"

Casper's cross-cultural giftedness with Pantene led him to apply the same insights to breathing new life into the Vidal Sassoon hair care line. Although the brand was aging in the West—indeed, the man who gave name to it had not even cut hair himself in more than 20 years—P&G felt there may be untapped potential in the East, especially Japan and its conspicuous consumers of luxury goods. Casper determined that the brand positioning needed to center on two important local values: heritage and quality. Age may be viewed as a liability in the West, but it is honored in the East, so "we unapologetically accentuated that respect, admiration, and history that Vidal Sassoon had represented in both England and the United States," Casper says. "The Japanese culture feels so much respect for age that it equals wisdom. They call a wise elder *sensei*—a teacher, a master. So we repositioned Vidal Sassoon, from being the product of an elderly stylist who hadn't cut hair in 20 years to one from this 'master,' and it turned out to be a fantastic success in the high income areas of Asia."

Lest he be tempted to make sweeping judgments about his cultural insights, Casper was reminded about how subtle cultural differences can be, when it came to developing packaging for the line. Aware that the Japanese are "fastidious" about their packaging, Casper proposed a striking, burgundy look for the new Sassoon Red Line—a sharp contrast to the traditional brown packaging in North America. "But therein was one of the big ahas," he says. "Unlike Pantene, where healthy hair and shiny hair were universally attractive to every culture, with Red Line price was more relative. "What is a salon in China or Bangkok or Malaysia is different than what a salon is in Los Angeles or Tokyo. We found the Red Line launch was especially successful in affluent markets like Japan, Hong Kong, and to a lesser extent the large cities like Shanghai and Beijing—places where people could aspire to this vision. "But to somebody in Manila or in Kuala Lumpur—where their connotation of what is a salon might have been a 10 foot x 10 foot room with a sink and a person with a pair of scissors—Sassoon was too far out of reach." So, while Red Line did well in Japan and Hong Kong, it fared less successfully in other parts. Returning to the U.S. in 1998, Casper was to find the lessons he learned overseas applicable here.

After three years involved with global strategic planning for laundry care, and 16 years into his P&G career, Casper left the company for the makers of Arm & Hammer and Trojan, Church & Dwight, where he served as President, Personal Care. He was recruited to become President and CEO at the Dial Corporation in 2005, which had just been acquired by Henkel, a German family company. When he arrived at its Scottsdale, Arizona, headquarters, Dial was "this scrappy survivor and challenger company—it didn't have the great brands that a P&G or a Unilever had, but it had some good brands like Dial and Purex. At Dial/Henkel, Casper had to draw upon his 17 consecutive years of working in multicultural, multinational enterprises. Dial's process-averse, "make-it-happen" culture was in stark contrast to its new owners, where process and discipline were held in highest regard. "I was able to draw immediately upon what I had both done and also seen while I was in Asia," Casper says. "I looked at how to synthesize what was effective about the indigenous culture and marry it with the best attributes of the parent company. My leadership (at Dial) was to provide structure where less existed. It's similar to what I did when I moved into China. China was growing but didn't have many formal systems. We needed to apply 'seatbelts and guidance systems' to help our rocket reach its target." At Dial, "I felt this weird sense of déjà vu, stepping into a strategic position for Henkel, nine time zones removed from its headquarters in Düsseldorf—similar to when I was running Hong Kong and China Hair Care (for P&G), 11 time zones removed from Cincinnati. Once again I found myself in a position of leading a strategically important subsidiary torn between two divergent cultures—trying to balance global guidelines with local imperatives. As the Chinese proverb says, 'The mountains are high, and the emperor is far away.' And that was how I approached things in Scottsdale as well. I needed to keep this company lean and fast moving, while creating a culture of innovation where none had previously been present."

Casper also drew on another P&G insight for his leadership at Dial. Leaders at P&G—whether...Ed Artzt, John Pepper, A.G. Lafley—"were gifted orators," Casper says. "They overcommunicated. During times of change, during times of restructuring, or transition, you always got a strong leadership voice coming from the P&G CEO. When I took over at Dial, I tried to emulate Pepper and Lafley with the quality, transparency, frequency, and personal nature of the communication. That is the key to success, particularly when you're asking people to transition themselves from being one way to being another. You set the clear expectation, and you constantly show people what great looks like." The lesson Casper learned is one that can apply in this country and around the world.

16

Kay S. Napier

Saying that Procter & Gamble (P&G) values go to the bone with Katherine (Kay) S. Napier isn't just a figure of speech. It's also a way of summarizing the crowning achievement of her 20-plus years with the company, when family heritage, professional development, and personal fortitude fused in a groundbreaking development. As head of North American Pharmaceuticals for five years through 2002, she led in a hands-on way the development and introduction to market of Actonel. Actonel protects women from osteoporosis, the decreasing bone density that accompanies aging and can leave them more at risk from fractures and attendant health issues. For Napier, the daughter of a devoted physician, there turned out to be more than inherited family concern about wellness. It became very personal. For, during the project, Napier found herself being prescribed Actonel—after being diagnosed with breast cancer.

Taking just a handful of sick days during her chemotherapy and radiation, Napier drove Actonel to one of P&G's most successful launches ever, reaching $1 billion in sales in record time. That was even more remarkable given that the drug was following an already established osteoporosis treatment, Fosamax, onto the pharmacy shelves. To achieve that catch-up and overtaking, Napier drew on some of the lessons she had learned in her earlier P&G years to bring Actonel up to speed quickly. P&G had actually pioneered the use of bisphophonates in treating bone disease but had been beaten to the punch in winning Food and Drug Administration approval for its use by Merck's rival Fosamax. Napier ordered a two-pronged response to the challenge. She recruited around 50 volunteers from P&G's pharmaceutical R&D and trained them to go out and present Actonel's clinical superiority to top leading doctors. Then she reached directly to consumers by partnering P&G with retailers like CVS and Walmart to offer bone density testing. The twin results: greater public awareness of the need to prevent and treat osteoporosis, and heightened acceptance by physicians of an alternative treatment.

The first step involved addressing an area where P&G superiors admitted to her the company had fallen short—a positive rapport with the influential medical community. Merck had most doctors' ears, "We jumped right in and started building a relationship with the top thought leaders in the world, and that relationship endured through the whole eight years I was in pharmaceuticals," Napier recalls, "and frankly had a lot to do with our success."

The second phase centered on an advertising and marketing campaign focused on consumers that earned *Wall Street Journal* coverage and one of P&G's top global promotional awards. Napier remembers the strategy for the way it broke out of P&G's typical business silos to bring different brand interests together. "We worked really hard to figure out what was the true benefit that was going to resonate with consumers, and it was really preventing that first fracture from happening, because once you get that first spinal fracture, you're kind of too late," she says. "I knew I really wanted to leverage the company's strength with consumers, and we were off to the side in pharmaceuticals. The company had this great relationship with leading retailers, and I partnered with Gordon Brunner, SVP, and Chief Technology Officer, who was extremely supportive of the concept of divisions working together on this initiative." The idea was to create a women's health and vitality platform, bringing together diverse P&G products under the umbrella. "It was not easily sold in the company at first, because it went across divisions," Napier says. But the results were impressive, not only establishing Actonel but playing a significant role in P&G's corporate rebound after some soft years.

CHAPTER 16 • KAY S. NAPIER

Having gone on from P&G to leadership roles at McDonalds for four years, and most recently as CEO of Arbonne International, LLC, a multilevel marketing skin care and cosmetics firm, Napier credits her P&G years as giving "more of an education by far...than I got in any traditional educational institution, because it was more rigorous, more intensive, more real life. The great thing about Procter is there is very little formal training. It's mostly on-the-job training, and from day one, you're taught that you own the project. Don't be looking for someone else to blame; it's your responsibility to get it done," she says. "And you also learn that everything's within your power to sell if you know your facts and have passion for what you believe."

But the learning curve can be steep, as Napier discovered when she spent three years in Germany as Marketing Director and Category Manager for Personal Cleaning and Deodorants. As an American who did not speak the language, and the lone woman at her management level, it was "the most difficult thing I had done in my career by that point." There were some differences that had to be worked out. "Like, Americans have a much more affable style, and sometimes it gets misinterpreted. Europeans are a little more formal and more guarded in what they might say, and I had to get used to their style...they had to get used to my style type...and we often met in the middle."

One area where she felt at a distinct disadvantage was not knowing German well. "I could never know enough to really go out and work in the field, with the retailers, and I always felt that that put me at a disadvantage...Even in the advertising development, I'd be looking at storyboards that were in German that had to be translated. "It was a great training experience for me...Going through all this adversity makes you stronger, makes you tougher. When I came back (to the U.S.), I felt like I was a much more capable leader and manager, because I had been through that." Although it was not easy at the time, Napier looks back and sees her time in Europe typifying what she believes to be one of P&G's great strengths, that "from the moment you start, you're given big projects...Over time it just gave you a sense of confidence that you would get through it because the company had faith in you to do it."

Napier credits much of what she experienced at P&G with equipping her for her current role as CEO. "I never would have been prepared for it had I not been in so many situations at Procter where I'm going, 'Whoa, I've never done this before, kind of scary—and then you did it with success.' There are a lot of things about being a CEO that I could have felt very insecure about, but I've never really felt terribly insecure. A little scared at times, but I figure I've learned enough in my career to get through it. When I went into pharmaceuticals at P&G, I wasn't a scientist, but people would say, 'Are you a doctor?' No, it's just that you figure out that if you just boil it down to the few things that need to get done—which is what you learn so well at Procter—and you focus on getting those done with excellence, you can get through most anything."

At Arbonne, that meant leading the business through and out of Chapter 11 in record time—just 37 days—despite dealing with multiple law firms and investment banks. "Where did I learn that kind of project management and leadership? Of course, I learned it at Procter," she says. Napier was "trying to get a bunch of people to move in the right direction. I felt like we were watching paint dry, and then when we emerged it was faster than anyone else had ever done. I attribute to P&G my ability to get through something like that that I had never remotely experienced with success—I really do."

From her time with McDonalds, where she was instrumental in turning around business by leading the launch of the premium salads and the global healthy lifestyle initiative that helped rehabilitate the company's unhealthy image, Napier came to realize that "there's more than one P&G way to get the job done." But "I also learned that there's more the same than different in a good company. If you ask me which of those jobs prepared me better for running a company, absolutely my Procter experience—without question. I couldn't have done it otherwise. I couldn't; there's no way I could run this company without having had that." Napier pays tribute to the way P&G fosters commitment and excellence: "It's indoctrination like nothing you can experience anywhere else. I mean, it's your family. You live in this environment of excellence. The kind of people you work with, they are great people. They're smart people, and you just aspire to do everything to the Nth degree, the right way." Those relationships—with "really smart, dedicated people, who are inherently good people but who strive for excellence"—transcend time, place, and even employer. "These people, you know them for life," she says. "I am still very much in touch with a lot of my peers from P&G, and I reach out to them for help in this job."

Napier believes the principles they share transcend geography and language. Returning to Procter in the U.S. from her Germany appointment, Napier also brought back an awareness that although cultural values and principles may differ, corporate foundations were essentially the same. "There were some nuances...For example, I didn't get that the whole privileged nature of legal correspondence didn't exist in Germany," she recalls. "I'd be saying, 'You can't put this in writing; you should put it in writing this way,' and that was a totally different legal structure. So you'd run into little things like that. But I'd say 90% of it, once you got past the cultural exterior of the various country behavior patterns, the fundamentals of the company were pretty similar. And that is another example of what P&G did: They gave you a world as a stage to learn how to be a better executive and leader within or of a company—and for that I am very grateful."

17

Cheryl Bachelder

Good leaders need to know where they want to take their businesses, but they don't have to know all the details of the route—just who to ask for directions. It's all about having a healthy sense of humility, according to Cheryl Bachelder, who credits Procter & Gamble (P&G) with helping her lay the foundations of her business career and later build it up through two influential times with the company. The first was in her three formative years right out of school, as an Assistant Brand Manager in the bar soap and household cleaning products division. She hadn't been looking for a job with P&G, but she was intrigued when the company came after her on the strength of the initiative and leadership she had shown in reestablishing a faded sorority while at Indiana University. "The highest order value that I learned from them is to take very seriously the selection, hiring, and then coaching and development of talent," she says.

At P&G, Bachelder absorbed fundamentals she exercises to this day. She remembers "how rigorously they developed my business skill set. You went through classes on how to run a meeting, how to write a memo, what a budget was, what a business plan looked like, how you tested things. It was the most rigorous, on-the-ground training you could hope for." Bachelder points to P&G's famed emphasis on memo writing, which she says wasn't just about procedures but more importantly was about the importance of effective messaging of strategies and ideas. "It was extremely rigid," she recalls of the memo protocol, "but one thing it taught you was that the first two sentences had better ask for the order: 'This memo is to get approval for what?'" She is grateful for "the messaging training that I got there, the rigor, the attention to how you structure your proposals and how you win people over to strategic ideas. "It's fundamentally different than what you learn at other companies, because now I know that most people—and even most executives—don't have that skill. But it is an immeasurable part of leadership to know how to message your ideas."

Bachelder also appreciates P&G's commitment to developing its people. "I don't think I've ever seen a company as focused on talent development as P&G," she say. As one of 60 new hires, she was "very green, but they took my development very, very seriously." Looking back, she sees that emphasis on the individual as P&G's "living out a value of saying we take time with our people, we develop our people. And even people that they exited, I saw them do it with complete integrity for the individual. I saw that you could fire someone and leave their self intact, coach them to a better fit opportunity and leave them thinking working for P&G was a great thing, no matter what."

Those were some of the core lessons Bachelder took with her when she departed in 1981—not for another opportunity but because her new husband, a fellow P&Ger, left the company to attend Harvard Business School. ("I would probably still be at P&G otherwise," she says.) Following three years' brand management with Gillette, Bachelder switched to the food world. She served as General Manager of the LifeSavers Division of RJR Nabisco before successful tenures, in turn, with Domino's Pizza and KFC. Since 2007, she has been CEO of AFC Enterprises, Inc., the franchisor of Popeyes Louisiana Kitchen restaurants.

Bachelder came full circle, in some ways, in 2009 when she joined the P&G Agile Pursuits Franchising, Inc. (APFI) Advisory Board. She applauds the founding of this group to help P&G develop its franchise businesses as "a very novel thing for a company of P&G's size and stature." She traces the move as coming from the second big impression P&G made on her. Bachelder feels the APFI advisory board was born out of an evolution in P&G culture brought about by A.G. Lafley. She recalls him speaking at a P&G alumni gathering fresh into his CEO role, asking how the company could tap into those who had gone on to see success elsewhere to help make the company better. "I thought that was a stunning moment in the history of the company," Bachelder says. Up to that point, P&G was a rather insular company, she recalls, "and he broke them out of that mold. Every Alumni meeting since then, the senior executives of Procter & Gamble come and they don't just show up and do a speech. They mix and interact and act interested in leaders who have left and it has benefited their company. The person who heads up their developing technologies, Jeff Weedman, is always at that meeting, hunting for entrepreneurs with patented technology that P&G could put to work. I mean, how big of an idea is that? It's huge."

Bachelder also gained a lot from P&G's ego-free atmosphere. The company had leaders "whose names weren't in the papers," she says. "They grew up from humble beginnings; they weren't all from Ivy League schools, pedigreed and credentialed. It was a humble environment for developing leaders, and you were encouraged to lead for the benefit of the enterprise, not for yourself. It wasn't a place that held up these towering self-centered leaders; it just wasn't cool at P&G to be that. In fact, most of those types got spit out like bad gum at P&G. That is a huge part of my leadership mantle today: to stay humble, open to input—that it's about the enterprise, it's not about me." Bachelder's favorite quote is, "It's not about you." That is the first sentence in Rick Warren's best-selling *The Purpose-Driven Life*. "I use it all the time," Bachelder says. "I say to people, 'You don't have to read the book, but you have to get this embedded in your forehead, that it's not about you.' I firmly believe that that cultural value is in place at P&G and that it shaped me as a leader."

As part of the APFI advisory board, Bachelder is one of three executives with franchising experience who meet once a quarter with the business leaders at P&G's APFI organization. "We give advice. We're there in an advisory role, but the teams present their business strategies and they invite us to bring our experience and our think-ing to bear on those strategies, and the coolest thing is they listen—they listen intently." She notes how Dimitri Panayotopolous, P&G's Global Vice Chair who is renowned for his international experience, including helping open up China for the company, asks questions. "He's a phenomenal global strategist and thinker, and yet he will ask us, 'How would you establish your rules of the road around the size of a franchisee?' And then he sits there and he listens for our answer, and I just find that a remarkable culture—where everyone from the Brand Leader of the Mr. Clean car wash to the Vice Chair of P&G is tapping into expertise that lies outside of their company and genu-inely values that feedback."

Bachelder has her own "kitchen cabinet" advisors at Popeyes and recalls Domino's Pizza founder Tom Monaghan similarly seeking out advice—his Advisory Board introduced him to Cheryl, and she worked at Domino's for the next six years. "His willingness to accept advice and bring people close to him with real expertise led him to strategy, led him to talent, and then led his company to a period of strong same-store sales growth." Bachelder is applying the same approach at Popeyes as she looks for rapid international expansion in the next few years. "I do not have on-the-ground, in-country international experi-ence," she admits. "I'm okay with that, because I've learned this lead-ership lesson of 'go find that experience and listen to it.' So we've just gone on a search and hired an international board member. He's now in my kitchen cabinet."

Bachelder describes herself as a huge proponent of the idea that "my leadership capability is unlimited if I'm willing to accept help from people way smarter than I, way more experienced than I, and I plan to make that a success strategy, not just for me personally, but for my company. I have tried hard to never get too proud or too worried about what other people think, to allow smart people in to give me counsel, whether it's setting strategy or hiring the right talent. Other people with different and broader experiences than my own have proven extremely valuable to my decisions as a CEO." This kind of approach is best from the get-go, not as a rescue plan, she says. "The right time to seek advisors is in a good time on your business; it's in advance of a strategic opportunity," she says. "A lot of leaders are too interested in appearing confident and in control to go out there and seek and accept counsel, and we see that playing out in the business world often in colossal failures."

In her current role, Bachelder believes that "the greatest privilege of leadership is to embed healthy values in the culture of an organization—and that comes straight out of the P&G mind-set and the way they go about doing business." Bachelder says that there was a period when "P&G demonstrated that you can't become a sleepy organization and be successful; they kind of learned that the hard way in the pre-A.G. Lafley days." She attributes the company's resurgence in large part to Lafley's "towering strength" which, she believes, was in leading innovation. "He opened up the channels for a far-reaching way of going about innovation that included outside parties—and that was huge."

18

Bob Viney

Perhaps no single story captures the essence of the strength of many of Procter & Gamble's (P&G's) values more than the twisting and turning one that tells how the company breathed new life into its flagship brand at a critical point for the business. In just a couple of years, a blend of globally sourced technology innovations, heightened collaboration, and risk-taking leadership snapped Tide out of a decade-long sales sleep and dressed it for fresh success—going on to become the company's first billion-dollar brand.

Bob Viney had a close-up view of the process as an integral part of the team that came together to enact P&G's belief that brands don't have to die. Although others in business see a natural four-step life cycle for brands—launch, growth, maturity, decline—P&G has always contended that new life can be found. But that seemed a stretch in the early 1980s, with Tide sales stagnant for a decade after leading the laundry detergent market since its introduction in 1946. The oil and gas shortages of the 1970s, raising the cost of the petroleum-based chemicals used in Tide, had prompted a focus on cutting formulation costs. But that led to reduced cleaning performance, which had always been Tide's competitive advantage. Meanwhile, environmental concerns—with blooming algae in the Great Lakes being attributed to the large concentration of phosphates in waste water, some coming from powder detergents—had raised the profile of liquid detergents that did not have the challenged chemicals. This was good news for rival Lever Brothers, whose liquid Wisk had all but owned the younger liquid detergent category for its ten-year or so history.

Era, P&G's entry into the market, had always struggled to compete despite being cheaper to use, because it had a lower recommended amount of product usage per wash. It was to this double detergent challenge—falling share in powder and failure to gain traction in liquid—that Viney was introduced when he was appointed the new U.S. Brand Manager for Era in 1982.

By then six years into his career with the company, Viney was tapped for the new leadership team on the struggling brand, which provided him the opportunity to leverage his experience marketing the new liquid enzyme product technology in Japan. As Brand Manager there for the company's liquid detergent, he had led the successful introduction of the new liquid laundry detergent, Bonus. P&G leadership hoped that a new enzyme-based formula being developed for Era would help its growth. As product development, manufacturing, technical packaging, marketing, and sales leaders came together on the project, they shared a key discovery from lab and consumer testing. Liquid detergents may not clean as well in regular washes as powders—with the challenged phosphates—but they had cleaning advantages when they were applied directly to stains as a pre-wash treatment.

Viney and the others saw an opportunity here, focusing promotion on Era's strengths and repackaging it to emphasize this newly realized benefit. Instead of the traditional cap, they proposed using a new, smaller push-pull top that could serve up pre-treatment levels of the liquid. The plan seemed to have floundered here, when P&G leadership turned down an appeal for the investment needed to produce the new caps. But what Viney calls the "get it done" mentality of the team led to a breakthrough, as Dick Antoine, who was heading up the P&G manufacturing plant in Lima, Ohio, where the Era group was based, came up with a solution.

One of his staff found a discarded push-pull capping machine in another P&G plant, brought it to Lima, and successfully installed it. Instead of having to spend heavily on equipment, the team had found what it needed "pretty much just for the cost of a plane ticket to Kansas City," Viney recalls. However, there was a contender for the kind of promise being shown by Era. A.G. Lafley, then a P&G Brand Manager, was leading another team that was hard at work elsewhere in the company, also exploring the world of liquid detergents.

This alternate liquid detergent formula was the output from the new Global Technology organization within Product Development. They were charged with the task of establishing a series of "World Projects" in the top six product categories, two of which were in laundry..."World Liquid and World Powder." These programs had the stretching goals of providing noticeable product and packaging superiority in the eyes of the consumer, to not only P&G's existing brands but the leading competitive brand in each relevant market. A further goal was that the resulting products and packages would have a global intent for utilization in the developed markets of the United States, Europe, and Japan simultaneously. Product Development and Technical Packaging teams were set up not only in Cincinnati but in Brussels, Belgium and Osaka, Japan to develop the World Liquid product and package. The new "World Liquid" detergent formula developed for the United States was designated as H-85. Formula H-85 was showing great promise, combining enzymes for pre-treatment stain removal with a new, non-phosphate ingredient that cleaned almost as well as phosphate powders in lab testing. This combination of effectiveness and environmental friendliness seemed to ensure a strong launch for the proposed new liquid brand.

Although P&G famously points its teams outward, on the consumer, making the shopper the main focus of decisions, within the company walls interbrand rivalries have long been acknowledged, if not encouraged, to some degree. Brand competition is part of the culture that stimulates growth and develops leadership skills in its people. But as Viney and Lafley began to talk about their respective brands, they came to the conclusion that the launch of a new liquid brand—offering Era's pre-treatment promises with the additional, cleaner chemical content, but with a half-cup recommended usage per wash compared to Era's current quarter-cup usage—might not provide a strong enough consumer-perceived difference to justify the large investment required to launch a second liquid brand. Lafley made a surprising recommendation to senior leadership: That they scrap the idea of introducing a second liquid brand and instead use H85 for upgrades to Tide and potentially Era.

The senior management in the division and the company agreed. "Not everyone would have made that decision," says Viney as he looks back, having eventually left P&G after 23 years to become an executive business coach. Given what he recognizes as "the competitive nature of brand managers," Viney credits Lafley's "maturity and focus on what was right for the business."

Not that everything was going to be easy. Yes, the new formula had a lot going for it, but it also required a half-cup measure—twice that of the existing Era. Yet, given the investment made in the H-85 World Liquid product, the Era Plus launch just had to succeed. The marketers decided to address the possible challenge caused by the different measurement requirement head-on, focusing on the message that consumers "just use a capful." That, in turn, demanded an effective measuring cup be added to the package. Several attempts to come up with a suitable cup failed. Instead, the packaging development group headed by Phil Carter, decided to look into creating a package that integrated the measuring cup and the cap into a single unit. Standard caps simply would not do; consumer feedback was full of grumbles about how the sticky liquid could not easily be rinsed from the threads inside the cap, leaving drips down the side of the packaging.

Packaging design group members came up with an innovative solution. They produced a cap with the threads on its outside, creating a combined cap-and-measuring cup piece. Next, they added a locking collar in the bottle, a pour spout and a "drain back" area that funneled residual liquid back into the bottle. The development was a huge success, scoring a massive 95-5 preference over the existing cap designs, in consumer testing.

With content, packaging, and promotion resolved, Viney's team moved to final, consumer testing ahead of a test market launch. They decided that, in addition to existing Era, Wisk, and Dynamo—another rival, Colgate's liquid detergent—the newcomer should be run against Tide, even though as a powder, not a liquid, it was not really a comparative product.

Although technical cleaning research had not found liquid Era Plus to fully equal Tide Powder, brand marketers thought that if consumers rated Era Plus anywhere near to Tide, they would have something to work with for marketing purposes. Viney says that the subsequent results saw "all hell break loose" at P&G, according to one team member. Era Plus not only beat all the other liquid detergents in the consumer ratings, it even topped Tide—for overall preference and cleaning results. The findings were so bewildering that further testing was ordered to make sure that they were not some kind of fluke. When the second round produced the same results, senior P&G leaders backed the next turn. What had previously been viewed as "heretical," Viney recalls—extending the long-standing and trusted Tide name into the liquid detergent market, and with a product that wasn't technically equal to its powder version—became the plan. Era Plus became Liquid Tide, "in a single day," says Viney. This decision to thrust the Tide name into the world of liquid detergents was not without its own risk, however. The potential damage of flanker bands cannibalizing sales from existing products was well known not only in the business world at large but inside P&G. Crisco shortening, the baking staple dating back to the early 1900s, was negatively affected by the introduction of Crisco vegetable oil in 1960. That kind of history left concerns for Tide Powder as Liquid Tide debuted. Would the stalled old guard lose even more ground, to an insider upstart?

Would that development make it even more difficult for the Brand and Division to achieve their financial goals? And how would Liquid Tide impact struggling Era?

In an effort to ward off the kind of defensiveness that could spark internal company tensions which might leak out in the forms of what Viney calls "defensive spending" on advertising and promotions, the responsibility for successfully coordinating the growth of both the Powder and Liquid Tide brands was given to a new Associate Advertising Manager, whose name was A.G. Lafley. This brought Lafley back full circle to the new liquid product he had championed, by giving it away to another P&G team. At the same time, a new Brand Manager was appointed for Tide Powder in late 1993, reporting to Lafley. That was Bob Viney. Galvanized by the unexpected success of the Era Plus-Liquid Tide thread of development, P&G saw fresh hope for Tide. CEO John Smale put long-term advertising agency Saatchi & Saatchi on 60 days' notice, ultimately concluding that ten years of no growth for the brand meant a major overhaul of its public face was needed. Viney felt that he would get better results working hands-on with the agency as it strove to come up with something new, rather than waiting to evaluate whatever it brought to him. He spent two full days at the agency's office each week. Figuring that starting afresh with a new Agency team would be a lengthy process, "I saw my role as doing everything possible to help the Saatchi & Saatchi team succeed," he says.

Drilling back down into what had made Tide the leading powder brand for so many years, the Saatchi & Saatchi team developed a new message that spotlighted the product's recognized cleaning superiority in a compelling and memorable way. The new advertising campaign launched early in 1984, with a playful story of a girl secretly borrowing one of her older sister's favorite blouses after being refused permission to borrow it. Disaster seemed to have struck when the top got stained—until a Tide wash saved the day. "Tide won't quit till clothes come clean" became the message that struck a chord with consumers, sparking its resurgence. Building on that momentum, Viney's team followed later in the year with the national launch of the first new Tide product since 1948—Unscented Tide. Although it had been successfully test marketed some 18 months previously, the product had for some reason never been rolled out further. When it was eventually debuted nationally, it quickly gained market share. With the brand starting to gain some traction again, Tide product development efforts were given closer attention. Historically, separate teams had worked on new technologies and proposed enhancements. But with the new impetus for the brand, they agreed that working together to come up with an integrated sequence of developments commercializing the next several product developments made more sense. It was also time to go back to some roots and take another look at the original Tide Powder box package, originally developed in 1948 but still in use. Inspired by the inventiveness of the new cap developed for what became Liquid Tide, product development team came up with a new pull tab opening that closed better and kept out moisture. The scoop that was added to the box was another plus for consumers, who gave the new powder packaging high marks.

With Viney leaving the Tide brand at the end of 1984 to help launch P&G's business in Taiwan, responsibility for continuing the growth of Tide Powder concurrently with the rise of the new Tide Liquid brand fell to a new Tide Brand Manager, Bob McDonald, P&G's current CEO. Successful product and packaging innovations matched with newly creative marketing proved to be a dynamic mix. In the following four years, combined powder and liquid Tide business doubled from $500 million to become P&G's first billion-dollar brand. The numbers are not the only measure of the successful Tide turnaround, however. As Tide's once-flagging powder and new liquid brands gained favor in the following years, Colgate—second-tier detergent rival, to Lever Brothers—eventually exited the U.S. laundry business, in 2005. Lever Brothers followed suit two years later.

Tide had gone from being a plateaued category pioneer to the sole-surviving king of the hill. "Brands are ageless, when a company commits to invest in its development and improvement, consistently over time," Viney notes as he looks back. Among the lessons, he sees that it is possible to fundamentally reshape a market when you have what he calls "the transformational innovation" that changes the basis of competition, because it offers to the market "a fundamentally different value proposition." Additionally, Viney says that "empowered individuals are capable of amazing results, especially when they work in highly collaborative team environments without an internal 'power struggle,' because it's the consumer who is in charge." And, with a nod to Lafley that should also note his own part in all that happened, he adds: "Breakthroughs and breakthrough innovations [that] change the norm in the business must be visibly led and championed by a leader willing to take risks."

19

John Costello

The main principles that have guided John Costello through a varied business career were shaped during a season at Procter & Gamble (P&G) in which, appropriately, the company had to comb out some of its own long-held essentials. The reflection and refocusing were prompted by a major effort to breathe fresh life into what had for long been one of P&G's flagship brands, Head & Shoulders shampoo. By the time Costello was appointed Brand Manager in the mid-70s, and charged with helping lead the turnaround, the shine had gone off. Head & Shoulders' anti-dandruff properties had earned it top market share following its introduction in 1961, but the world and hair care changed in the next decade-and-a-half. People were showering more regularly, dandruff was less of a problem, and soft, healthy hair was more of a concern. Some consumers were worried that a treatment shampoo like Head & Shoulders might be more than their hair needed. As a result, the brand had been in a multiyear decline when Costello got his assignment after three years at P&G.

"It was a little daunting," Costello admits. "It was a highly visible brand in a rapidly changing category...We really found ourselves drawing a lot on the values and core principles that I had begun to learn as a Brand Assistant and Assistant Brand Manager." Looking back, he identifies three essentials that were crystallized by the Head & Shoulders challenge: focus on the consumer, make the most of your team, and never forget the importance of brand differentiation. Those three things have remained at the forefront of Costello's thinking since leaving P&G in 1983, after 12 years, for Senior Executive roles at Pepsi-Cola, Yahoo, and the Home Depot, before becoming Chief Global Marketing and Innovation Officer of Dunkin Brands, the home of Dunkin Donuts and Baskin Robbins, in 2009.

"First, it all begins with the consumer," Costello says of the Head & Shoulders challenge. Although the brand was still the market leader, with a clear benefit, "the consumers' view and habits in the shampoo category were changing so rapidly that the apparent need for that benefit was being reduced dramatically and the category had begun to move to more beauty-related brands. So, the first thing we had to do was make sure we really understood what the consumer wanted and where Head & Shoulders fit." That prompted the formation of a cross-functional group, bringing others from research, product development, sales, and consumer affairs alongside the brand team "to set about understanding what consumers wanted and what did we need to do?" Their research confirmed that consumer attitudes had shifted and that what had once been Head & Shoulders' strength, its treatment capabilities, were now, if anything, more of a liability. Costello was persuaded that "the changes occurring in the shampoo category were fundamental and not merely a fad." His team concluded that the answer was "new product, new packaging, new positioning with new advertising, a new sales promotion plan, and a new public relations effort that was really designed to respond to the changes in the consumer marketplace." In other words, it meant weaving a completely different style from the same threads.

Such a radical shift required buy-in at multiple levels—hence Costello's second key lesson: "the importance of people," he says. "As a young Brand Assistant, your success is often determined by your own personal productivity. But as your portfolio broadens, you come to the realization that your ability to have an impact is influenced by your teammates as much as anything you would do. That includes not only your teammates on your brand, but your key partners throughout the rest of P&G. There's an old saying that's one of my favorites,

'There is no limit to what you can accomplish or how far you can go if you don't care who gets the credit.'"

The third lesson Costello sees in the Head & Shoulders turn-around—with the reoriented product going on to regain its market dominance—is the importance of knowing what sets a brand apart from others. The Head & Shoulders project pushed leaders in P&G to look hard and tease apart variables and nonnegotiables: What is a fundamental element of a brand, and what is merely the best way of positioning it for a period? "Because it was the leading brand, there was a reluctance to walk away from its historical brand differentiation" centered on its anti-dandruff capabilities, Costello remembers, "even though the market was changing rapidly. There's an important lesson here: While you may introduce a brand to meet a specific need, you also need to make sure that you are evolving your brand to respond to the consumer need."

Although Head & Shoulders was "well managed" within its increasingly narrow niche of treatment shampoos, "all of the growth in the category was coming from the beauty-related and nonthera-peutic segment. It's an example of where the consumer habits and practices were changing rapidly, but there was a reluctance to tamper with the historical point of difference." Costello is sympathetic with the hesitation. "There was an honest debate about whether the brand should continue to try to win within the therapeutic segment or whether broadening the vision of the brand would diffuse its reason for being. I think you have to approach combination benefits very cautiously, so I think it was an appropriate question: Were we, in fact, updating the brand, or were we walking away from our clear point of difference? How do you update your relevancy without walking away from the core of the brand...We were coming to grips with a funda-mental strategic question."

Reversing the long-standing Head & Shoulders decline earned management applause, but also raised a question about how that growth would be sustained. "That reinforced the lesson that building a brand is a marathon and not a sprint," Costello says. "The challenge was not just could we reverse a five-year share decline, but could we truly position the brand for long-term growth?" The answer was to be an emphatic yes, with Head & Shoulders going on to become a powerhouse, billion-dollar brand for P&G. "Balancing short term and long term is important," Costello notes. "It's important to hit your annual sales and profit goals, but it's even more important to plant the seeds for a long-term healthy business." Having since worked in more nimble business environments, Costello says of his Head & Shoulders experience that the biggest challenge of that kind of major reevaluation of a brand is in balancing speed and thoroughness. "A hallmark of P&G's success is its thoroughness," he says, "and that thoroughness can sometimes slow things down—which can be a problem in a market that is evolving rapidly."

Costello also appreciates his mentors at P&G, Bob Wehling and Bill Connell. "They instilled the need to be thorough but not to be afraid of taking risks," he says. "The personal interest they showed in me really set an example of how important it was take an interest in other people. Both were very demanding business people, but I always felt that they trusted me and wanted to do the right thing, so when they challenged my recommendations, I always felt it was to make things better. They led by example, and I looked at the impact their interest in my development had, and it really showed me the impact I could have on others when helping them."

Although his career has taken him to different corners of the business world, he says, "I have found the value and core principles of P&G are just as relevant. The key is to translate the values and principles of P&G and not attempt to duplicate all of the tactics. Every business is different, with different consumers, different dynamics. You need to think how the core principles of P&G may apply to different situations and not be reluctant to modify them."

20

Fernando Aguirre

Fernando Aguirre may make the principles for success sound simple, but that should not be confused with them being easy. When he says that it all boils down to building on common sense, hard work, sacrifice, and passion, his answer belies just what that can demand. But the depths to which each of those foundations must be driven can be traced through his 24-year career with Procter & Gamble (P&G), in which he established a reputation as a turnaround specialist marrying business excellence with personal determination and commitment.

Much of what he still draws on as the Chairman and CEO of Chiquita Brands International was forged in four challenging years in Brazil, starting in 1992. The Mexican-born Aguirre went to the country as General Manager, after joining P&G from college where he had a baseball scholarship. He rose through the company's brand management ranks. P&G had entered Brazil three years before, acquiring another business. It was known that some things needed sorting out, but no one realized the extent of the problems until he arrived.

"In my first three weeks, I learned that it was a disaster," he recalls. "P&G had bought a company that had sales of about $70 million, and they were losing about $40 million. Now, how do you lose $40 million in revenues of $70? That's the situation I faced." And headquarters "had no clue." Once he had a handle on the extent of the crisis, Aguirre went to see his boss, Jorge Montoya, who oversaw P&G's Latin American operations from Caracas. They laid out the true, bleak picture to CEO Ed Artzt and President of International John Pepper when the men visited two months later.

On a flight to Brazil, Artzt asked Aguirre for his plan. He had worked on it diligently, proposing the losses be slashed by half the first year, to $20 million, then cut to $8 million in the second, with the goal of breaking even in year three. It was ambitious—or so Aguirre thought.

Artzt "looked at me and said, 'I like your plan—but I want you to do it in one year.'" Artzt told him that he didn't want the company to lose any more money like it had done with its entry into Japan, over a painful ten-year period. "So think about a one-year plan and let's talk about it tomorrow at the meetings," Artzt told Aguirre. The directive came as the group arrived in Brazil for meetings with the subsidiary leaders. "So we landed in Sao Paulo and I went home," Aguirre remembers. "I started to look at my three-year plan and making adjustments and cuts here and there, and 24 hours later, we were in front of Artzt and the staff entourage and we talked about it." Needless to say, some functional leaders were unhappy. "Of course, every function wanted to keep their people...Ed looked around and said, 'Okay, I like the plan and I want it done in one year. And for the rest of the people, I want all of you to know that Fernando has all of my trust and I have given him the accountability and responsibility for the Brazilian results. We will do whatever he says we should do.' And he looked at me and said, 'Fernando, if you don't believe that you're getting the support you need from any of the staff people in this room, you call me directly and I will deal with it.'" Having backed Aguirre, Artzt then also told him, "We're going to do your plan, but you got one year. And I mean a year—if you don't think we can do it, you let me know and we will just exit Brazil and we'll send you somewhere else."

Looking back, Aguirre credits Artzt with "giving me all the confidence in the world to succeed, without really knowing a hell of a lot more than just the plan that I had presented to him. At the time, I didn't realize it, but I couldn't have gotten a more powerful statement from the CEO of the company...I had all the power passed on from the CEO to me." It was all the encouragement Aguirre needed.

A year later, the P&G venture in Brazil broke even, the second and third years it made some money, and by Aguirre's fourth year, revenues were around $450 million and profit was higher than $40 million, and Brazil had become the second-largest subsidiary in Latin America in both revenue and profit.

Aguirre sees his Brazilian experience as formative not just for what he learned about leadership from Artzt, but what he had to learn on his own. He could not have been further from the center of the P&G universe, yet the lessons were more valuable than sitting in Cincinnati. Ever since, he recommends to anyone looking to grow that he or she actively seek a similar challenge away from headquarters. More than training, he sees this experience as a transformation. "I learned the most in that assignment in Brazil, for several reasons, mostly because of truly having responsibility of a business for the first time by myself," he says. "In every other job I had, my boss was a few steps down the hallway. The Brazilian job was my first experience as a leader of an organization where my boss was 5,000 kilometers away."

Montoya was available for counsel on the phone or on visits, but otherwise "I had the opportunity to really apply my knowledge from my training and realize what I didn't know, and at the same time realize what I had to learn. To this day, those continue to be the most important four years of my professional career, because that's where I really grew up and learned how to be truly a leader of an organization. I discovered, learned, and absorbed from people, trying different things and taking some risks—things that you don't do until you're left out there by yourself."

He advocates to anyone looking to get ahead, "Ask for an opportunity to be sent abroad somewhere, where you can be by yourself, running a business—your own business." Most of P&G's North American leaders, he notes, are based in the company's Cincinnati hometown. "Their bosses are a few steps away, and no matter what they tell you— and I was there and I was one of those—you just don't do or learn the same things or practice the same leadership when you're by yourself.

Think about it: If your boss is a few doors down, you know there is a safety net; your support is there, and you know that there is someone else who can make the decision for you. While it is much more difficult to make decisions when you know your boss is not down the hallway, you also learn faster and get to see results right away."

Aguirre's Brazil posting required long hours, and it exemplified the other traits he believes are crucial for success: hard work and sacrifice. He doesn't buy the idea that it is possible to build something big with a nine-to-five mentality. "If you want to succeed, you want to achieve big things, then you have to work long and hard. I have told my kids that many times and they joke about the Blackberry being on the table during dinner, lunch, and holidays and so on, but they know if I didn't do that, I just couldn't succeed in my job."

Although he remembers Brazil with emphasis, his time there was only one stop in a notable P&G journey. Joining the company in Mexico in 1980 as a Brand Assistant, he worked his way up to Associate Advertising Manager before being called to Cincinnati, Ohio in 1986. There he served as a Brand Manager of Oxydol and of Hispanic marketing for PS&D. From there it was to Toronto as Associate Advertising Manager for Laundry and then back to Mexico City as a Country Manager for Laundry and Cleaning.

Aguirre was promoted to General Manager of Laundry and Cleaning in Mexico before being sent to the Brazil post. From his success there, he returned to Mexico in 1996 as Regional Vice President of Latin America North and Regional Vice President of Laundry for Latin America. Three years later, Aguirre moved to Cincinnati once more, as Global Vice President for Food Products, before becoming President of Feminine Care. His last P&G role was as President of Special Assignment, reporting to CEO A.G. Lafley before he left the company for his own new challenge as CEO of Chiquita in 2004. As he looks back at his P&G career of almost 24 years, he believes the biggest lesson he took with him was to "learn to manage with values and principles in mind. P&G is an organization that teaches you very basic core values and principles from literally the first day you walk in the door, and they don't let you forget that you have to make all your decisions on the basis of very strong values and principles."

"They have adapted them and changed them somewhat over the years. However, P&G is very specific and disciplined about making sure people are very conscious of what is the right thing to do for the consumer, for the employee, for the long term, and very importantly, doing what is ethical...They expect every employee to abide by the law above everything else. They remind you of that every single time they can, from the very first day on the job to the very last day at the company. And that, to me, is the most valuable lesson from P&G: to make decisions on the basis of values and principles. Once you leave, you see the real world is full of people who attempt to break or circle around principles and values that other companies have."

Aguirre's early days at Chiquita reminded him of his time in Brazil. "Very similar," he says. "I had no clue of how to be a CEO. We were trained to be General Managers, and we were trained to make decisions with values and principles in mind at P&G. But you don't have CEO training or CEO school until you get the job, and you learn it's very lonely at the top. The hardest part is to deal with the tough people issues." Aguirre also applauds the training he received at P&G, together with an appreciation that although personal effort is critical, so is the role of the team. At P&G, he learned "that you work with a heck of a lot of very capable and very bright people [who] are so critical for the success of the company, and there are so many people around you who are well trained, very skilled, and do their jobs very well."

Aguirre's simple and final piece of advice to others looking to make an impact is to be passionate. "I said it many times, as long as I can remember at P&G, when I got my first responsibility for people as a Brand Manager, and I say it over and over again to this day. If you drive to work every morning and you look at yourself in the rearview mirror and say, 'I hate to go to work, I don't like my job, I don't like the people I work with,' then that's the day you ought to walk in, resign, ask for a different assignment, or look for something else to do." Aguirre says, "If you don't love what you do, you're in deep, deep trouble. What I've learned, and have tried to pass on to my kids as well, is that you have to have passion for what you do. And if you don't have it, that's the first sign that you're either in the wrong job, or the wrong career, or the wrong company, or the wrong business. The good news is there is only one person who can correct that: you."

Part IV
Core Values Drive Vision

21

Sam Solomon

Sam Solomon may not have been with Procter & Gamble (P&G) long, but he considers his time there seminal, strengthening, and what shaped the raw materials he brought to the company for his subsequent career. In some ways, P&G was the anvil on which Solomon's personal ore, mined from a vein of strong family ethics and personal adversity, was further heated and hammered into form.

He has leaned on the core values honed during his short years with the company "over and over" in various settings since. They are so ingrained "it seems like I've had them forever." Solomon was slightly older than many P&G newcomers when he arrived upon graduation from business school in 1992. He came with military service and had the life-altering experience of losing a young son to leukemia. That background, along with the encouragement his parents had always given him to seek to make more of himself, prepared him well for P&G. The value, he says, that "really stands out, and the one I find myself leaning on over and over again" from his P&G days "is this notion of constant personal development and constant development of all of those around you, and not being at all intimidated about what you don't know, while having a thirst to go figure it out."

That P&G lesson echoed one from his parents, who had left their farming community in North Carolina to pursue educations and a better life. As Solomon was growing up, his parents sent him back to work relatives' farmland each year to help him learn that "no matter what you think it is, your situation could be worse—and if you're smarter, your situation can be better."

Solomon found that emphasis of continuous improvement interwoven with a complementary, second essential foundation at P&G—a commitment to doing the right thing. "This sense of integrity was born out of the fact that so many employees of P&G, and certainly those in senior management, were folks who had incredibly long tenures inside of the company," he says. "I understood the reason and the need to have integrity: People need to be able to rely on you and anticipate what you're likely to do."

The P&G emphasis on integrity resonated with Solomon personally, but he did not see until later how it played out practically, too. "I didn't realize that despite leaving the company and perhaps changing roles that you will continue to run into the same people again and again, and having a rock solid integrity that folks could rely on would be equally valuable outside of an environment like P&G as it was within it." Now, he says, it's a business basic: "You're going to see folks again, you're going to see customers again, and you're going to see suppliers again." He knows that there are really no shortcuts and that if something sounds too good to be true, it likely is. "People who suggest that if you do this, we can get you a swimming pool in your backyard, or wouldn't you like to have this car...all those things just raise a red flag and make me wonder if these are the people I want do business with. And the answer is a continuous, no. If they're willing to cross this line for me now, what lines will they cross that are not in my favor, later?"

Solomon believes that P&G's commitment to team, the importance of the consumer, and the product over the individual in the company fosters the need for integrity. "I am a firm believer that no one of us is smarter or more capable than all of us," he says. "To me, integrity is that solid backbone in a high-performance team where, when someone on my team takes a chance, makes a decision, I have to know that they've done that with the highest integrity—I have to know that they've put in the work with all of the data available and they made the best choice that they could at that time."

Solomon credits the mentoring he received from his first boss at P&G, Wendell Clark, Director of Paper Cost Analysis, in shaping his future leadership style. As a Cost Analyst for Diapers, Solomon was responsible for coming up with the annual budget, following the company's model. "It's several billion dollars worth of numbers you're playing with," he recalls, "but the magnitude quickly wears off." He was pleased with his work when he took it in to Clark, who checked Solomon's report thoroughly and agreed the numbers were all correct—but then dropped his bombshell. He said, 'Well, what happens if pulp goes up a penny?'" Solomon had no answer. Nor for what would happen to his figures if resin went up a penny. Solomon remembers Clark explaining: "You're going to be in a meeting, we're going to get information that's going to change a significant element of the model. Everyone will know it has a major impact, and the meeting will stall unless you can authoritatively say that impact is $10 million."

Clark advised Solomon to go through his numbers again, running them with a change in price for everything from plastic to glue. "He told me, 'Write all of that stuff down and memorize it and do it every month. Now, if you hear that there's a change in prices in a meeting, people flip out and start to stall, you simply can estimate real-time that a penny change in this commodity is worth $7.5 million.' He taught me not only the notion of getting the model right, but anticipating and having an obligation to allow the general management team of that business to keep moving forward while everyone was gathered, so that rather than being concerned about the magnitude of a change, they would be reasonably confident that they knew what that magnitude was and could keep the strategic discussion going without it stalling."

Solomon says he learned from Clark that "the output was not the objective. I had a model that could estimate cost, could do it every month, could estimate the year, could estimate the quarter with fairly high degrees of accuracy, frankly. So what? He viewed that as just an input. "Because when you're done generating these numbers, you're going to give them to someone else. You need to anticipate what that someone wants the numbers for, to try to answer the question that's on their desk."

Solomon looks on the principles he holds fast to as a sort of internal compass—an appropriate metaphor for someone who headed famed outdoor company Coleman for several years. He went there as CFO and Vice President of Administration in 2005 after post-P&G positions that included Coca-Cola. Solomon took over as Chief Executive Officer at Coleman in 2008, leading the business until 2011, when he left to join Sears as President of its tools business.

The idea of an inner compass "means a constancy of purpose on the one hand, and then a constancy of a direction on the other hand," he says. But Solomon also knows that "there is often some sort of magnetic interference that gets you turned around and gets your compass off a few degrees, so you've got to correct and head back and align yourself again—with strategy, with the principles that make you successful. While you can have a certain direction, it doesn't mean you won't have to detour a bit in order to actually take yourself or your organization there." The kind of "magnetic interference" that can take you off-track "is usually transient," he notes. "You're passing through something, or near a power line, or whatever. Corporations look like that when teams get overly focused on the short term without regard to what are the longer-term implications to any decisions." It is particularly true for those in public companies, he suggests, pushed to perform for the next quarter's report. "That desire to put up short-term results, we all have, but if you do that in a way that doesn't take into account your longer-term direction, you find yourself spiraling downward. You make another set of short-term decisions to make you look good and, unfortunately, you find yourself overwhelmed and very often in a place where you're going to have to do something extreme to get out of the ditch—and often that's a tempting place for you to compromise your values."

Solomon acknowledges being "very keenly aware" of what he calls the 90-day contract—the need to put up good quarterly numbers.

"But I try to do that in a way that is consistent with my ultimate direction. Even if there's no clear line of sight as to how I get there, I have got to go in the direction that's the correct path." While on the subject of compasses, Solomon says that the old-fashioned needle kind—symbolizing someone's personal "true north," their own inner convictions—can at times be preferable to external help from the latest high-tech gadgets. That could also relate to relying on others or outside sources. When that modern GPS is working, it's hard to beat, he says. "But go through an underpass or get yourself in a canyon with tall buildings around, and you can lose your signal. If you didn't plan your route or you don't have a general image in your head of where you're trying to go, you're dead in the water." His point: "Just because it's easy, it doesn't take away the need to understand where you're headed, and generally how you're going to get there."

22

Steve Case

Although the steady and measured approach to business development that has been Procter & Gamble's (P&G's) hallmark and heritage may seem to stand in sharp contrast to the faster-moving demands of some emerging markets in the 21st century, one pioneer in the new realms credits his time with the company for at least some of his subsequent success. Steve Case, the man who helped bring the Internet to the masses, paving the way for seismic changes in the way people interact and buy, sought out P&G to help prepare him for the future.

Freshly graduated in 1980 with a degree in political science, an entrepreneurial leaning, and a curiosity about the potential of developing technologies, Case chose P&G as the place to learn about foundational principles and processes. "I recognized it was a large company, but also a great marketing company and a great training ground. I went hoping to learn a lot about business generally and marketing specifically," he says. "And that is what happened. It was a great experience and important stepping-stone to some of the other things I went off and did later." During two foundational years with P&G, Case started as a Brand Assistant for Toilet Goods, in Cincinnati, got promotion sales training in Atlanta, and then earned a position as an Assistant Brand Manager. Among those he worked with was then-division leader Bob Herbold, with whom he would later compete as leaders of rival technology giants.

Case points to a couple of the key lessons he learned at P&G. "It really was and is a terrific company, particularly strong on marketing and the business development as well as in people development." He learned a lot about "just being thoughtful in gathering information, market research, focus groups—a lot of testing." Through his involvement with a couple of new products and introducing them in test markets, he saw the importance of "the process of trying to understand what consumers were thinking and what products they would likely embrace or what features would be important to them, and the whole process of being fairly disciplined in terms of testing different hypotheses, was important." Another key point he picked up was "the idea of communicating concisely and clearly about your thinking and your recommendations in the form of a one-page memo."

Case also appreciated the way the company gave responsibility to young staff and trained them to be managers and leaders. "I was always impressed by the fact that it really was a company that promoted from within. P&G recognized that it was able to attract people to Cincinnati because of the power of the company—but in order to keep them there, they really needed to give them opportunities, give them responsibilities, give them new skills, so they would want to stay with the company."

When he arrived in Cincinnati, Case sensed that his tenure would not be long. "Even as I went to P&G, I already was fascinated with the idea of what would become the Internet, and so that was always in the back of my thinking," he admits. "So I went there knowing it was a great company, expecting to learn a lot—and that was certainly the case—but I didn't expect to stay too long." There was an unexpected side benefit, too. When he was there, Cincinnati was a test market for one of the few interactive TV experiments in the country, Warner Qube. "It gave me the opportunity to see this interactive world begin to unfold, even though it was an early precursor of what's emerged over the last 30 years or so."

Case also tucked away lessons for his future endeavors from what he saw as the downside of a large organization. "Being in a large company like P&G, that was so successful and had such strong brands, a lot of it was about trying to protect the franchise and extend it through incremental improvements, and I recognized that, by definition, those large companies move relatively slowly," he says. He recalls test market projects where "it would have taken a year to understand what the impact of a very slight difference in pricing or packaging might be." Fast-forwarding to his time with AOL and more recently his investment firm Revolution, he says of P&G that "the strength of big companies can also be their weakness—which is the deliberate approach they bring to bear...They are defenders, trying to protect the status quo, not attackers, trying to usher in new concepts. Understanding how large companies think and act helped inform my thinking as I started developing AOL, and those lessons have also played to the entrepreneurial companies we've been building at Revolution."

Although he chafed a bit at the slow speed at which he saw P&G move, he appreciated the emphasis on "having to make things really simple for consumers and a compelling, easy-to-understand kind of unique selling proposition...and also the process of generating trial— for example, giving people samples of shampoos—with the hope that if they tried them, that would lead to an ongoing purchase habit." All of that played into AOL's early success, he believes. "We really tried to understand, I think more than some of our competitors, what consumers were thinking, particularly the mass market we were going after. We weren't focused on the technologically sophisticated and Silicon Valley people; we were focused on the general population, trying to get Main Street America online, and as a result some of that P&G thinking and training served me well."

Case sought to replicate P&G's "trying to be crisp in what the key benefits were—knowing that simplicity matters, and sometimes 'less is more'—and then communicating the benefits clearly and convincingly." He also tips a hat to P&G for the hallmark AOL effort that he is teased about even now, a "very aggressive sampling strategy" that saturated the market with trial disks. "In the early 1990s, when we felt the Internet was poised for rapid growth——it was about to shift from being a niche hobbyist market to becoming a more mainstream mass market—we flooded the country with free trial disks. We gave the AOL software away for free and gave people a free month to try the service. That helped propel AOL's success. It is fair to say my early training at P&G was instrumental in ingraining in me the importance of using sampling to drive consumer trial and adoption."

Case acknowledges that he was in some ways an unlikely fit for P&G, dialing down his natural risk-taking bent for a more "corporate" approach. "It was an adjustment for me. My DNA was about being entrepreneurial and moving quickly and nimbly. P&G forced me to slow down and be more systematic and disciplined in my thinking," he says. "I started with those entrepreneurial 'attacker' instincts and had to train and discipline myself to fit within the P&G system." When he left the company for a year with Pizza Hut before in turn heading to Washington, D.C., and what would become the forerunner of AOL, he was able to "get back on a trajectory and track" that was more of his rhythm. Case tolerated a high degree of uncertainty and tried to divine where things were going and then reacted quickly to technological and consumer changes as well as competitors.

Case's desire to not just make money but to make a difference was "an evolution." In his 20s, he says, he was more focused on building his business, although even then "I did believe that the Internet could change the world by empowering people and giving them new tools. That became kind of a bedrock of the vision of AOL, really trying to make the Internet as ubiquitous as the television or the telephone, but more valuable. So I was always focused on a higher calling, if you will, and some of that was because I really believed in the power of the Internet, as a new medium and a new force in society. We wanted to communicate that it was a big idea. It was not just about what you saw today, but it was how it was going to evolve. As a company, we were collectively working with AOL's members to build a medium we could be proud of."

Just as some of what he learned at P&G bore fruit in AOL—where he competed with Herbold's Microsoft for online supremacy—some of what he came to understand there, through the company's merger with Time Warner, he sees woven into his developmental work with Revolution. "Some of the lessons learned in terms of building AOL and building the Internet as a medium, we're now trying to apply at Revolution in different sectors of the economy, including health care, financial services, and transportation. So for me it really is a logical next step."

He views the last 25 years as "the first Internet revolution," building the technology, the platform, and the audience. He expects the next quarter century to be the second Internet revolution, "as it becomes a force of change in almost every aspect of people's lives—including how they stay healthy, how they get educated, how they buy things, how they move around, and so forth...Revolution builds on some of the core ideas that drove AOL." He traces threads from his P&G days through it all. Whether it's democratizing the Internet through AOL or challenging transportation norms through the Zipcar car-sharing service Revolution is backing, he says, "There are some similarities, in terms of trying to keep the consumer proposition simple, really focusing on the key areas of differentiation, making it easy and inexpensive and sometimes even free to try it, with the idea that it creates potentially a lifelong customer. It's partly the values but also some of the business and marketing principles, I think have applied in these new areas, even though these new areas tend to be, by definition, more disruptive, risky, uncertain, unproven, and for me that's really been what's been fun—marrying the desire to do these interesting, disruptive, change-the-world things and the desire and preference to be able to be nimble and move quickly, but also coupling them with an appropriate level of structure and discipline and thoughtfulness."

23

Kevin Roberts

As a passionate rugby fan, Kevin Roberts appreciates the importance of being a good team player, but when it comes to business, he believes that another group identity is more foundational: family. The marketing maverick—remembered for machine-gunning a Coca-Cola vending machine in one of his presentations while leading rival Pepsi Cola in Canada—sees the family providing the foundational values of commitment, loyalty, trust, and respect on which Procter & Gamble (P&G) has built its business and reputation.

"What I learned at P&G was the importance of family; that family beats any other sort of communal noun that you can think of," he says. "It beats a team, it beats a tribe, it beats a community, it beats an institution—if you can feel like a family, then you will win. I learned that family values mean demanding, yet caring, and it's the caring part that's terribly important. P&G cares about their people. Samir Hawwa told me early on, 'Promote three things—promote your business, promote your people, promote your boss, and you'll do really well.' And that's really been at the heart of my leadership beliefs ever since."

The lessons he learned during seven-and-a-half years with P&G have guided him through a globe-trotting career in the past three decades. At 32, he became the CEO of Pepsi-Cola, Middle East. He moved from there to take over the company's business in Canada and secure a note in publicity lore for his Coke machine stunt. In 1989, he moved to New Zealand to become Chief Operating Officer with brewer Lion Nathan. Seven years later, he became CEO of renowned advertising agency Saatchi & Saatchi, overseeing their 150 offices around the world—and finding himself "back in the family in the best possible way," servicing leading P&G brands.

Roberts credits the fatherly trait at P&G that gave room for young talent with ideas. "We don't have a lot of cynics in Procter & Gamble. We have radical optimists, and they take pride in what their subordinates and the people underneath them are doing. P&G has this family view that, perhaps you'll make a mistake, but as long as you learn and fix it, that's what families are all about. You have the comfort and the security of the family—P&G allows you to fail, because in the end, it's about the idea, not the person, and people will...help you get back on track." That doesn't mean there are not failures, he emphasizes, but "there's not a blame culture in the company. Instead, there is a lot of fail fast, learn fast, fix fast. 'Let's interrogate the data; let's get the personalities out of here. Let's all go forward together.' That's the way families deal with problems."

He recalls how P&G's family values were reinforced for him while trying to help build market share in Morocco in the late 1970s, working for Herbert Schmitz, who he describes as "dynamic, entrepreneurial, and incredibly inspirational." As marketing director, Roberts wanted to step up from the toehold the company had secured with Tide, to introduce the likes of Pampers, Crest, and Head & Shoulders.

In a country with no big supermarkets and lots of mom-and-pop stores, he felt that it was important to "go in and dominate the trade." Although the tactic was not in step with the P&G principle of "consumer as boss," Schmitz agreed that the approach might be effective. The pair presented the idea to Sami Sherif, and "he tore into me at a million miles an hour," Roberts remembers. "He said, 'What you're suggesting, all the sales, promotion, and trade pressure, and dominance, might make business sense, but it is not the way we do business at Procter & Gamble. The way we do it at Procter & Gamble is we put the consumer first; we put innovation first.'"

Schmitz defended Roberts' proposal, "and they had this big ring-ding argument where Sherif in the end, said, 'I've said everything I want to say on this. You guys, you're running the business. Go away and decide what to do.'" Roberts and his superior went away "and decided that we better listen to this older guy; he's pretty smart. The lessons of that to me were that a principle is only a principle when it costs you money, because I still think my plan would have made more money faster but...." He learned "about how in brotherhood, your boss and you go into battle together and you sink or swim together." He values the way P&G offers wise counsel to younger personnel but also gives them room to make decisions. "They won't order you. 'I've told you this; it's up to you now to go ahead and figure it out for yourself.' I also learned humility," he says. "You know, he was right, over the long haul. I don't know if that's a story I'm proud of—it makes me look a bit of a monkey—but it's one that I feel in many ways goes deep."

Looking back, Roberts learned from P&G that great companies "are driven by a purpose that is much bigger than simply selling product and meeting consumer needs. P&G has got a purpose to improve the lives of people throughout the world, and that's been a very important lesson to me: starting with purpose, not with brands, not with companies, not with R&D, not with innovation; it starts with purpose."

His years with P&G didn't just fashion Roberts' leadership beliefs; they forged his understanding of effective branding—captured in his influential books *Lovemarks: The Future Beyond Brands* and *The Lovemarks Effect: Winning in the Consumer Revolution*. Roberts says: "Most of my 'Lovemark' thinking was rooted in what I learned from P&G...trying to create loyalty beyond reason. That's at the heart of Procter's whole marketing; loyalty beyond reason, beyond price, beyond benefit, beyond attribute." For example, the brand he most loved in his time with P&G was Tide. "Tide has nothing to do with laundry. It has everything to do with family—it has everything to do with who your mom is, and who you are as a mom, and who your kids are. You can talk about cleaning and you can talk about dirt removal until the cows come home—Tide's a 'Lovemark,' and Ariel is not, right? Because Ariel has been driven by functional benefits, enzymes, science, technology, and is the best laundry cleaner in the world, the best stain remover. Tide's been driven by cleaning you can count on, by being a great mom, by remembering who you were...and Tide is a much bigger brand than Ariel. The story is right there."

Roberts sees the same thing in other products. Olay "is a brand that has moved from being functional, performance-based into 'love the skin you're in,' a beautiful transition from functionality to 'Lovemark.'" Pampers "was all about dryness, all about health, and now it's all about well-being and baby development. Classic move."

Head & Shoulders' early focus was all about the way it dealt with dandruff, he says. But it is now one of the two best-selling shampoos in the world, "because it's got out of just dandruff and into use every day. It smells great, makes you feel great, makes your hair shiny. It hasn't made the complete transition yet, but it's on the journey."

Arriving at P&G from Gillette, where he had been Senior Marketing Executive, Roberts' career had started at the Mary Quant fashion house in London in the late 1960s when Britain's miniskirts, mods, and mop tops shook off the country's starchy image. Viewed as "sort of a wild guy," Roberts appreciates that P&G's clear-cut style and approach still left some wiggle room—just as families can accommodate individuality. "90% of the success of Procter & Gamble is about doing the right thing all the time and really doing the hard jobs relentlessly," he says. "But there is room for inspiration and innovation and risk, and I was always encouraged in that when I was there. I brought in a belief in creativity and coupled with a bias for execution, which the company valued, they didn't try to make me something I wasn't."

As an "outside-insider" during his P&G years, working in Europe and the Middle East, Roberts also developed a theory that drives much of his thinking to this day: that development often occurs at the edge of an organization, not necessarily in its center. "The further away you are from the center, the more fun you're going to have and the faster you're going to grow," he asserts. "If you study biology, you'll see that the development of most species is at the edge. So when you're in the Middle East, it was a lot more liberating than being in Cincinnati, where you have data, you have process, you have organization, and you have structure. We were out in the wilds, in the field, and so decision-making is faster and responsibilities are earned earlier. It's like the stories of pioneering and adventures P&Gers would tell in the 1930s in the United States, or when they first went to Canada. It's like the U.S. Wild West in 1880, really," he says. "That spirit still prevails. So the company is terrific, because it can handle the paradox of the discipline from the center, while still providing oxygen and freedom to ride on the fringes."

From his position working with the world's great companies, Roberts reckons that P&G "continues to set the pace," making it an attractive recruiting ground for other companies. If you can make it at P&G, you can make it anywhere, he says. "It's like New York, right? And the company is constantly innovating, experimenting, challenging, and reframing Brands and Marketing. It's still the best place in the world to work, learn, and grow...(and sometimes leave!)"

In the past few years, Roberts has noticed wider—if grudging—recognition that P&G's "consumer is boss" credo is on the money. With the advent of technology and social media, businesses have "got to understand that no longer do companies control brands. We live in a participation economy where we have to give up control of our brands. The consumer is the boss, and we've got to participate with her. We've got to stimulate her, entertain her, listen to her, take her advice, take her counsel, understand empathetically how she feels, and we've got to allow her to influence our brand, so that they can play an important role in her life. We've got to move from command and control brand marketing, to an unleashed and inspired model. We've got to have the confidence to give up control and, boy oh boy, companies find that very difficult."

One shift businesses need to make in this new world, Roberts says, is rethinking return on investment (ROI) benchmarks. "ROI is the wrong way to think about the world. The right way is to measure return on involvement; that's what we should be measuring, not your return on investment. That's so 1950s. We should be measuring how involved people are with our brand. How involved are they with our promise? How involved are they with our purpose, because today, if they're involved, they'll buy. They'll participate and they'll be loyal. If they're not involved, they'll just functionally buy a brand until they get a better option."

Looking ahead, he sees "everything I learned at P&G is going to become more and more true. First of all, you've got to become a trustmark, so you must deliver quality, authenticity, performance, functional benefits at the right price, everywhere the consumer is. That is job number one. Nothing. Nothing," he says, "is going to change that. The timeless truths of purpose-inspired, benefit-driven will never change. How we communicate and share them will change massively. What will be at the top is not the brand equity. What will be at the top is the consumer. So we'll go sort of upside down if you like, where the consumer is boss. And we'll add mystery, sensuality, and intimacy to our trusted brands, thus making them irresistible Lovemarks."

24

Jim McNerney

The fuel for Jim McNerney's turnaround leadership at Boeing can be traced back to the early days of his business career when, as a junior Procter & Gamble (P&G) staffer, he learned "you run toward problems, not away from them." That certainly describes his flight path since becoming CEO of the aircraft giant in 2005, plotting a fresh course for the company in the wake of a series of turbulent ethical scandals that had rocked confidence in the business.

Although he had significant leadership successes to look back on and draw from when he took on the Boeing challenge—including CEO posts at 3M and General Electric—his fresh-out-of-school experiences were just as top of mind. "You learn to remember at an early age what the business objective is," he says. "It's not to look good in a functional organization and avoid controversial issues. You run toward problems, not away from them. You're taught that at Procter & Gamble." Purpose and values and ethics "are core; they're not a behavior," he says. "You're as likely to be asked to leave Procter & Gamble because of issues around purpose, values, and ethics as you are around performance."

In many ways, the values McNerney was exposed to in his three years with P&G as a just-graduated Brand Assistant and Assistant Brand Manager, from 1975, were those he had grown up with. "What's right and wrong at home, what's right or wrong in your community, is equally right or wrong in a corporation," he says. "People used to think that right or wrong was different in a business than it is at home.

But it isn't. It's the same, and Procter & Gamble was a place where that was very easily understood."

The P&G commitment to doing the right thing was fostered, too, McNerney believes, by a culture that emphasized what really mattered in the end. "When you work in big companies, it's very easy—particularly when you're down in the organization—to not identify with what the objective of the company is...which is to gain market share, to drive profitability, to satisfy customers," he says. "P&G lined you up very nicely with that. There weren't internal politics that counted. There weren't relationships that counted. Things that tend to count in other places, they didn't count at P&G. What counted was how good a teammate were you? Was the team winning?" But you have to know the score to be able to celebrate if your team is ahead—and that requires "a business in which you can keep score," McNerney says. Like P&G, where "the business is broken down into brands and things where keeping score is facilitated at a very low level in the organization, and people own things deep in the organization, brands and winning count, and losing counts. That's a good culture."

McNerney recalls P&G's famed insistence on research and clear, concise communication of the results, to make the best possible decision attainable. "Balance, thoroughness, data, decision-making, is teachable, is learnable, and that's why you wrote the memo seven times," he says. "You know what work completed around decision-making looks like. You learn that at a very early age and you remember. You'd write a memo at least seven times, but you'd learn...it has the value of not only helping reach a better decision, but bringing everybody together around the decision, because you're taking the heat out of it and you're bringing rationale and logic into it. You're taking subjectivity out of it, and you're bringing objectivity into it, which is all about the way decisions got made at Procter & Gamble."

McNerney found himself falling back on his "Procter & Gamble memo" learning in recent days at Boeing. When his team faced a major decision, he composed a P&G-style summary for himself.

"Even though it wasn't my role to do it, it really helped me get my thinking together and got the team together," he says. "It helps a lot." McNerney appreciates how the P&G emphasis on analysis also encourages people to participate. "There's lots of meetings where one or two bullies—or people who have positions that outrank others—get very emotional on a subject. But if you create an environment where that doesn't count as much as who comes up with the best argument, you're going to run a better business. "That was some learning from Procter & Gamble."

Beginning in business at a company where principled decision-making was emphasized over internal politics and personal positioning "was a great place to start, because you learn what it's like to be in a place that doesn't have much" of the latter. "You learned to see it and smell it fast, because you were brought up not having it, and you're less tolerant of it, because some people come from places where it's an accepted way of doing business," he observes having since experienced different organizations. "I mean, apple polishing does count in some places. It didn't at Procter & Gamble. I think it helped me be a better leader because I learned to know what's essential and what isn't, and you don't feel like you have to put up with the stuff that isn't."

McNerney's foundational days with P&G not only prepared him for his later challenges, but have come full circle, with him joining the P&G board in 2001. One of the reasons he accepted a seat was "frankly, because I knew that this was a company of unquestioned integrity. It's one of the things that drew me to the company, quite honestly. It also leads to where you're unafraid to offer your perspectives, because you know everybody's reaching for the same goal, which is to do the right thing for Procter & Gamble. There's no hidden agenda."

McNerney's appreciation for the P&G way of deliberation also helps him guard against what he says can be a challenge for seasoned executives—letting past successes short-circuit opportunities to nurture up-and-comers. "You may give off vibes that don't encourage participation, because you already 'know,'" he says. "I think you have to work on that. You have to work hard to be inclusive, even when you're absolutely convinced you're right, because one of the most valuable things you give people who work for you is the chance to go through the process of learning themselves. But you only do that to a point. I mean, you can't spend all your time in a hot tub nurturing everybody all day long. You want to be mindful of finding yourself trapped in your experiences, and try to take the edge off it. I think it is important. I think it's something I have to watch out for, too."

McNerney offers advice to those looking to find their place in the business world: "First and foremost, make sure you're part of an organization that values performance, that values growth, and that is willing to invest in you. Not every organization is like that, and if I wasn't in a company like that, my advice would be to change companies, okay? Then, once they've done that, I would tell them to work their butt off and make other people better as they're achieving their objectives. I'm a pretty simple midwestern guy here: It's all about hard work, it's all about treating others right, and it's all about achievement. Winning counts."

25

Dean Butler

When most people leave an organization, they move on with their lives and typically leave their past company in their rearview mirror. For Dean Butler, the positive working experience, training, mentoring, and values instilled in him at P&G propelled him forward to lead incredible change in the optical industry. Dean founded Lenscrafters in 1983, and within only four years, it became the world's largest optical retailer. Butler leveraged the Procter & Gamble (P&G) value of challenging the status quo to redefine the vision care industry. Instead of focusing on adapting to external trends, he led a renaissance movement in the eye care industry where his teams shaped external trends over time. They were the very first optical retailer to promise eyeglasses in about an hour. Lenscrafters went on to perfect complete customer convenience by bringing an independent doctor of optometry, the optical laboratory, and a wide selection of frames together under one roof.

Butler's foremost goal was to establish Lenscrafters' core values that his entire team could embrace and build definition around. These values included team unity, winning approach, push for new ideas, accept mistakes, nurturing of talent, risk taking, ability to connect to people, demand highest quality, constantly improve, and have fun. It was Butler's vision to have all Lenscrafters associates and doctors live out these core values.

Early on, Butler was able to excite the general public around smart, yet revolutionary ideas. He simply didn't allow his team at

Lenscrafters to be put in a corner because of long-standing, industry traditions. Butler understood that his team had to educate public opinion for their ideas to take hold. Not surprisingly, the more successful they became, the more each Lenscrafters associate embraced the company core values.

Coming out of a culture that cherished market analysis, Butler used his marketing and analytical skills to rationalize a unique company like Lenscrafters. Looking across time and into what consumers really valued, he considered what the eye care industry was delivering to "patients" and what a new concept in retailing might deliver in the future. Once his insights were confirmed, he turned his trend watching into a business plan and launched Lenscrafters.

Butler says that "when a core value drives how your company serves consumers with the best product, the basis of this success typically starts with research and a strategic plan." Often paralyzed by too much information in the past, Butler streamlined his thinking and built a Lenscrafters plan that had few moving parts, focusing only on the big picture—complete customer convenience. The simplicity of his plan made it easy to understand for investors, and equally easy for his team to embrace and execute. He says, "Simply put—we would produce customers' prescription glasses in an hour or less, let them watch the process, and in doing so, demystify optometry industry secrets. Most importantly, we would create a whole new movement for consumers to have their vision corrected."

According to Butler, if you really care to provide the best product, service, and use of customers' hard-earned dollars, why not explore distinctive advantages and alternative ways of delivering product or service? From an investor's perspective, why not wait to invest in only those projects that close the product or service gaps that consumers are seeking? With Lenscrafters, Butler was able to show a clear vision on how consumers would benefit and how an old industry could be changed for good.

Butler admits that it is often easier to start your own company with your unique idea versus changing an existing culture that may be slowed down in the process. "Even today in the United Kingdom, companies are bogged down in being process-oriented versus a drive for results. Across Europe, there is an orientation to rules. In the U.S., the focus is on getting the job done with an element of speed while achieving the very best results." Standing for something greater than a product or service can also be the ultimate accelerator for a company. This is certainly the case with OneSight®...: Giving the Gift of Sight. Lenscrafters has sponsored this nonprofit organization since 1988, targeted to aid 314 million people worldwide who suffer from poor vision because they lack the means and access to proper eye care and eyewear. OneSight® was a tangible way of applying Lenscrafters' core values through reinforcing team unity, building on the company's winning approach, and connecting people on a worldwide basis to give the gift of sight. To the Lenscrafters associates and doctors, they truly lived out the company spirit by providing free eye exams and glasses to those in need around the world. Overall, Butler believes that Lenscrafters' market success was about the broad consumer's acceptance of the company's quality product and delivering behind the promise of glasses in an hour. "For employees, they identified behind our stated company values, mission and reveled in our company's success. Like P&G, we supported the idea that our financial success will not happen without our commitment to values.

When *Fortune* magazine reported on Lenscrafters in 1985, the headline read: "What is the difference between marketing eye glasses and detergent? Not much, according to Dean Butler." The success formula of finding a new strategic position, surrounding yourself with an excellent team, and advertising your message with exactness was worth repeating for Butler. How is having a clear vision a strategic core value? "Without a clear vision, how do you know where you are going? At Lenscrafters, we focused with single mindedness on the service in one hour or less. We treated patients like customers and hit as close to 100% of our production goals as possible. Similarly at P&G, we were limited to running three marketing test at one time. We used to challenge upper management on this perceived narrowness. Senior leadership would say do three markets and watch it work. Their experience over many years proved that keeping the market tests to a manageable level was a part of a long, successful pattern of success. P&G also taught you how to read the consumer and understand what was working or not. What works today for your consumers might not work tomorrow. You have to continually find out from the marketplace what your consumer desires. You can always count on things changing. When I started in Packaged Soap and Detergent, the laundry detergent competitors were getting innovative. Cold water products, new perfumes...you had to figure what your brand was going to do to be one of the top few brands. Back then, Tide was 'uncatchable.' We were all fighting for a 3 to 4 share. We constantly monitored results. In the laundry detergent wars, you learned that you can't be all things to all people. Are you going to have a product that softens laundry or gets grass stains out? You focused on one."

"In the eye glass industry, our target consumer is in the vast middle—not the high end or the low end. It was our intent to create uncontested market space and make the competition irrelevant. We wanted to create a substantive benefit (one hour) and provocative promise (never heard of that) and be believable (we actually made eyeglasses in about an hour). Nobody believed you could make quality lenses in an hour. We didn't put glasses in the window; we put the manufacturing plant in the window. At the end of our television commercials, we gave the consumer permission to believe in us. And putting all of our employees in white lab jackets...he would hear... 'look at all those doctors working on my glasses.' We were a pioneer in experiential retailing with this simple idea."

Leaning on his advertising wisdom gained at P&G—from the likes of Norm Levy and Dick McKinney... "brilliant guys who looked at marketing that worked in the marketplace"—he said, "we boiled down the success formula to substantive and provocative message while giving consumers permission to believe. Lenscrafters did not have to invent anything. It doesn't take but 12 minutes to make most glasses. If you are grinding a hockey puck, the stronger the lens, the less grinding had to occur. Most higher strength lenses are the least time intensive. The most difficult lens to make is one with no prescription or a very low prescription—because it has to be absolutely perfect. It's not rocket science to reposition a brand or product. In principle, step back and objectively look at that product and determine why consumers buy it...what [you can] do to make it better."

"With one of our core tenets calling for empowerment of everyone in our business," he says, "we gave every employee the duty to create enthusiastically satisfied customers. You should not have to go to your boss to make a decision that benefits your customer. Just do it. It was the cheapest advertising we would ever get. On top of that, one customer in five in optical retailing comes back with a problem, usually having to do with how the glasses were fitting...a problem easily remedied by any Lenscrafters associate."

Part of Butler's unique vision was never viewing anyone as a meaningful competitor. "Existing competition called themselves ethical optometrists. They called us commercial optometrists. Those ethical optometrists typically had inferior retail locations because they didn't think like retailers who are oriented to customers. In the UK, optics had just moved out of a national health service where everyone got free lenses. We introduced no-line bifocals. The established traditional optometrists said we were selling products, 'not clinical indicated.' We had learned that consumers in U.S. did not like bifocals with lines. We majored on more aesthetically appealing products, including higher index of refraction products that result in thinner lenses. The traditionalists did not generally offer these products since they thought it was wrong to be 'commercial.' Yet our customers would say, 'Why didn't my old optometrist tell me about this?'"

Butler is a firm believer that core values can help a company grow. "Look at Walmart; they had a core value of every person in the store being important. A huge part of their growth was traced to how smart they worked. At Lenscrafters, empowerment drove growth. We were making decisions in the customers' favor. Our employees felt that we trusted them to make a decision. We generally hired high school graduates who often did not have too many people to cheer them on. We saw to it that they were enthusiastic. For new store openings, I would tell them: "You aren't here today because you are going to get wealthy. You need a job, and we are going to create an environment of fun and family orientation. Remember, our core values include having fun."

"I encourage company leaders to articulate core values from day one. Don't be afraid to change your core values as your company evolves. Let me also encourage company leaders to on-board new employees with your own specific core values from day one. Have get-togethers (not meetings) where people are free to express their feelings. Hold special events like our Lenscrafters Lab Olympics, similar to McDonalds where they compete to see who can assemble a milkshake machine the fastest. Lenscrafters has their own unique competition to determine who can make quality lenses in the shortest period of time. At end of our Olympics, we asked participants how they can apply the lessons learned from the competition. As it generally goes, our best ideas came from where the rubber meets the road."

Dean Butler is carrying forth "the spirit" of high performance expectations from P&G, while leading with his own style crystallizes the Lenscrafters culture around the company's own core values. He is not about simply doing similar things in a new, improved way, but in creating sweeping change in an old industry.

26

John Pepper

The long-term achievement of companies, communities, or colleges is the result of a measured blending of principle, persistence, and professionalism—doing the right thing at the right time. John Pepper has a unique perspective of what is required for enduring accomplishment of this kind from his vantage point at the helm of three storied institutions.

The long-time Procter & Gamble (P&G) leader, whose nearly 40-year tenure included tours as CEO and Chairman of the Board, went on to leadership positions first with his alma mater, Yale University, and then the Walt Disney Company, where he is Chairman of the Board.

Each organization enjoys widespread respect for its longevity and recognized leadership in its own field, which Pepper attributes to the kind of shared values and foundations he first encountered at P&G. The issue of integrity, he says, is central to everything. Having a personal passion for "pursuing truth no matter where it leads" as a young student and at one time having considered a life in law, "nothing, absolutely nothing, impressed me so much as the integrity that I found at Procter & Gamble," he recalls. He recognized the company's focus, he says, as "an integrity founded on the commitment to the consumer, to try to do the right thing in all things at all times, to do what is right for the long term."

Pepper notes how principles get tested, though—such as the challenge Yale faced in recent times when wrestling with a 25% drop in endowments that required major budgets. But the school's leadership determined that, somehow, students' learning and living experiences would not be affected. "They wouldn't let that happen any more than P&G would accept dilution of product quality as a means to confront a financial challenge," he says. That kind of commitment to doing the right thing is one of the most important elements in the marrow-deep values that drive day-to-day decisions and actions of successful organizations, Pepper believes. Integrity is "a priceless attribute," he says a fundamental characteristic "of every great company or institution."

He says that the importance of a group's commitment to the growth and development of its people is something that has to be more than just a policy statement. P&G's promote-from-within practice "necessitates a relentless focus on recruiting and retention." As part of that focus, P&G has been "quite unique," Pepper thinks, in placing people in jobs with broad responsibility at a relatively early age.

That emphasis is an expression of the company's belief that everyone counts. Pepper quotes John Smale, his predecessor as CEO at P&G, describing the business's tradition of caring for its people as "perhaps the most important part of its character. If we ever lose that, if we ever stop caring about each other, we stop cooperating. If we stop caring about each other, we lose our common vision, our sense of purpose, our commitment to the success of our company. And should that ever happen, this company will no longer be unique among the world's business organizations."

Pepper says that Smale's view echoed an earlier leader, R.R. Deupree, whose declaration, "You could take away our brands and our money and our buildings, but if you left us our people, we could rebuild the whole thing in a decade," is quoted in present-day recruiting materials to inspire prospective recruits. Pepper acknowledges that he wouldn't want to have to put Deupree's assertion to the test, "but all of us know the truth he was getting at."

As he considers the three big institutions he has been part of, Pepper finds far more commonalities than differences. They are centered, he asserts, on two things: being a sustaining institution and being a community. The two "go hand-in-hand," he says. Pepper cites former P&G Senior Executive Mark Ketchum's recollection of feeling "incredibly well connected with the people I was working with... close in knowing what they thought and felt and what they had passion for. Close in the common objectives we shared and the dedication we had to achieving them. Close in the honesty and candor between us. Close in our belief that nothing could stop us—that our destiny was in our control. We shaped the culture that we needed to accomplish great things."

A shared purpose is integral to that dynamic, which for P&G "has always been about providing superior service and performance to consumers through our brands." Although it has been expressed in different ways through the years, the sentiment is the same. Pepper remembers then-Vice President of General Advertising, Ed Lotspeich, who Pepper came to know in his very first week at P&G in 1963, saying that "the consumer runs our business." Fast-forward to A.G. Lafley, his successor as CEO, whose assertion was that "the consumer is boss."

P&G's closeness to its consumers and the company's commitment to learn from them is unsurpassed, Pepper believes. Today, that customer focus is captured in P&G's "Touching Lives; Improving Life" mission statement. Such intent needs to be measurable, Pepper says. That can vary depending on the context. At P&G, it means "we live and die by achieving share growth on our brands, by achieving superior consumer satisfaction and increasing household penetration."

None of this would be possible, though, without "a burning commitment to innovation," he says. "It is a never-ending quest to keep learning, to find better business models, constantly improving, finding new and better ways to carry out and broaden the fulfillment of their purpose in light of changing consumer needs, technology, competition, and emerging global opportunities." For P&G, that means an ongoing series of organizational and process redesigns, Pepper says—among them, the establishment of the brand management system, the creation of customer business teams, developing a product supply organization, restructuring as a global company, new consumer research methods.

P&G's experiments with Tide drycleaners and Mr. Clean carwashes are examples of how it is exploring new business models, he says, and notes how, in similar fashion, Disney is launching schools in Beijing to teach English to young Chinese, while Yale is moving to create a university in Singapore. When a sense of overarching corporate purpose is alive in an organization, many of its people "don't feel they are just in a job, not even just pursuing a career," Pepper comments. "Rather, they are engaged in a calling."

At the same time, success for the organization depends in good measure on "extremely strong personal leadership at multiple levels," Pepper says, "starting with the CEOs." Among the qualities they need: "Bold vision, great strategic sense, focus of execution focus, team-building, and the ability to help people grow and the impulse and capacity to drive continued learning and innovation."

Pepper reminds us of the former P&G leader Smale's insistence that "it isn't enough to stay in business and be profitable. We believe we have a responsibility to society to use our resources—money, people, and energies—for the long-term benefit of society, as well as the company." Pepper sees that being achieved in different ways, including how Pampers' commitment to baby development is not only impacting design of its products, but helping provide vaccinations to save millions of babies' lives around the world. Elsewhere, he points to how revenues from Always pads are going to help provide education for young women in Africa.

Enduring success of the kind seen at P&G, Disney, and Yale also means never taking it for granted, Pepper says. "Always recognize the danger of arrogance and bureaucracy, and the importance of staying close to and respecting the consumers we serve and those we could serve," he says. "Never forget that, in the end, success is all about people and values."

Part V
Doing the Right Thing

27

Bob Wehling

It takes a clear compass setting and a strong rudder to keep a boat on course through shifting tides. Bob Wehling knows that well from having helped steer Procter & Gamble (P&G) through the peaks of global expansion and the troughs of adverse publicity in his 41-year career with the company. Both opportunities and challenges require a steadfast commitment to underlying values and principles, even as the way these fundamentals are played out, he says.

Take P&G's expansion into the Middle East and then the former Soviet Union, following the collapse of the Iron Curtain. "One of the issues we had to face, over and over again, was when our corporate values and principles differed from the values of the country we were entering. There were some countries where bribery was a given, as it had been for thousands of years. You didn't get your product shipped into the country without crossing the palms of customs people, retailers, distributors," he recalls. "Everybody had a piece of the action, and when we would say our principles don't include bribery and we're not going to do it, this created a hell of a challenge." In some cases, it required ingenuity to break a deadlock. The company would run consumer advertising creating demand for the products and ultimately put pressure on retailers and in turn the government to bring the products in. "Eventually, it all worked out, but those were difficult situations."

While overseeing public affairs and global marketing, Wehling was "involved almost weekly in issues where our values were different than the values in another country." Many times the clash centered on top-rated TV programs that delivered the best audiences for advertising, but whose content ran contrary to P&G's standards. "In Chile, the number-one program at one time was one that made fun of blacks with the iconic old black face kind of humor. We had to tell our people in Chile, much to their displeasure, that you can't be on that show. We simply were not going to be involved with programming anywhere in the world that denigrates a religion or a race. We're just not going to do it."

While managing P&G's television soap opera involvement for 20 years, Wehling was heavily involved in representing the company in the U.S. market. As the shows began to get more racy, some people questioned P&G's continuing association with them, especially in light of the business' conservative benchmarks. "People would say, 'You tell us you have these principles about not advertising on shows that are obsessed with sex, but yet you're advertising on the soap operas. How do you justify that?' I used to tell people what I liked about the soap operas was that they all followed the law of the harvest—that you reaped what you sowed. I never knew any characters on any of our soap operas who got away with anything. There was always a lesson and a moral—that if you do this, you're going to pay for it. It might take a year for your transgression to catch up with you, but it will catch up with you. Our viewers understood this, and it kept them attracted to the shows. They knew that Joe was going to get his just desserts, but they didn't know when it was going to happen."

One thing that has helped keep P&G on course, Wehling believes, is the bedrock conviction that decisions are made with the best interests of the consumer in mind. At no time was that founda-tional value challenged more than in the Rely case. Women loved the new tampons introduced in the mid-70s. "Based on all of our testing and research, it was by far the most absorbent product and worked better for them than anything then on the market," he says. When suggestions first arose that the tampons might be linked to toxic shock syndrome fatalities, "there was a lot of back-and-forth about what was causing it." Wehling emphasizes that when CEO Ed Harness made the decision to pull the product from shelves, "there was no good scientific evidence that Rely was the culprit. The decision to pull a best-selling product when there was no hard evidence that it needs to be pulled—but you're doing it just in case it's part of the problem, for the protection of your consumers—that's a decision you have to admire a lot. It was a principle decision as opposed to something 'we had to do,' and that's what I admire."

Though Harness' call was a brave one, in some ways, it was not a surprise to Wehling. "I was taught from early on that the company always tries to do what's right for the long term and that you should never make a short-term decision that could negatively impact the long term. That was drilled into me from day one, and we all grew up believing that," he says. "So whenever we did propose something that we thought was right for the short term, we always asked ourselves, 'Is this consistent with building the company and serving our consumer over the long term as well as being what we need to do right now for the short term?' It's just the way we thought, and it became a natural way of thinking and asking."

Still, applauding Harness' decision—which he considers one of the hardest in P&G's long history, costing the company "a hell of a lot of money"—Wehling reflects on the leader's personal leadership style and observes that when an organization has clear core values, there is room for different approaches to living them out. Harness and his successor in the P&G driver's seat, John Smale, "were very different in the way they approached the business, but they shared the principles and values of the company." Harness was "truly a people person," Wehling says, who cared deeply "about employees and the community and our consumers, but whenever he made a decision, he thought about the implications of that decision on people."

Wehling recalls the time when, as Brand Manager on Puffs facial tissue, he had recommended an advertising agency change. Wehling

and his boss, Ed Artzt, took the proposal to Harness. "Late one evening in Ed's office, I remember him looking out his window into the
night with his hand massaging his jaw while he was thinking. Ed rumi-
nated, 'Gosh, this is going to be a terrible blow to the two people who
run the ad agency. We were going to take the business away from
them.' He said, 'I just want to be awfully, awfully sure that there is
no other alternative here, that the problem is not some problem of
our own as opposed to a problem with the agency.' And we agonized
about it. We must have spent 90 minutes just talking every issue back
and forth and finally, he said, 'I hate to do it, but okay, go ahead.'
That's the kind of guy he was. He just didn't do things quickly without
a great deal of thought when people's lives, feelings, and livelihoods
were at stake."

By contrast, Smale was "much more of a thoughtful, numbers-
oriented, highly disciplined person," Wehling says. "Not that he
wasn't a people person, but most discussions started with the impact
on profit margins of the brand. Smale was a steward of the company's
well-being, and he wanted to ensure that we made enough money
to support further innovation, which he saw as key to our growth."
Both men were great leaders, "but very, very different in leadership
style. In fact, that's one of the other things I had always thought was a
strength of the company." Wehling notes how subsequent leadership
saw John Smale as "very disciplined and business-oriented," followed
by Ed Artzt, "a true global thinker," and then John Pepper, "another
people person like Ed Harness."

Wehling says that core values, common values, and principles
remain strengths for the company today. We could all get along and
respect each other while sharing common values.

Another strength has been the company's willingness to flex on
procedures while adhering to principles, being willing to take a risk in
doing what is believed to be the right thing. That was clearly illustrated
in the turnaround of Secret deodorant, one of Wehling's personal
proudest contributions at P&G. When he inherited responsibility for

the brand, it was a major money loser, so Wehling and his team proposed a drastic change. "It had such a bad reputation," Wehling says. "We felt that we had to do something to win people back and show them that we were different." The team advocated a rebranding of Secret that targeted women, with the slogan, "Strong enough for a man, made for a woman." As part of their proposal, the group also recommended a launch that ignored traditional business formulas. P&G liked its brands to spend their money evenly through the year, "but because of the radical changes we had made and what we felt we needed to accomplish, we went into that budget meeting proposing to spend 35% of the total year budget in the first couple of months. We were thrown out and told to come back with a more responsible plan." But Wehling was convinced the risky strategy was the right one and persuaded the others they should stick to their guns. "We went back into the second meeting with essentially the same plan," he says. "I knew I was at risk of being fired and taking a few teammates out the door with me, but I knew it was right for the brand." At the end of that second meeting, Wehling recalls, the review group told him and his team, "Well, we don't agree, but you guys obviously feel very strongly about this. We will go along with your plan and see what happens." Secret's subsequent resurgence proved Wehling's judgment to be right. As the Secret Team Leader, his name is synonymous with the brand's applauded revival, much as Smale will always be remembered as the man behind the success of Crest. "But there's never any one person who does anything at Procter & Gamble," he says. "It's always teams of people."

Through his involvement with P&G's television interest, Wehling was one of the founders of the Family Friendly Television Forum. His interest in issues relating to children and education have continued since retirement from P&G, with his director's post at the James B. Hunt Jr. Institute for Educational Leadership and Policy Development.

In addition to his celebrated role with brands like Crest and Secret, Wehling was a significant figure in encouraging and promoting diversity within P&G. When he started there, back in 1960, he says, "I think there was one woman in advertising. It was all a white male, white shirt, dark suit kind of an operation. We had a lot of difficulty adjusting our culture to accommodate women and minorities." Wehling identified and championed young woman and minority candidates while also encouraging change in the culture of P&G for "all the right reasons, not filling quotas. My belief was always that governmental quotas telling you who to hire don't work—at least I never saw it," he says. "I remember when the Equal Opportunity Commission was first created and we were told to do a better job of recruiting minorities, for example. Our culture embraced diversity when we experienced diverse teams producing better ideas and ultimately better results. That's what drove our ability to attract and retain both women and minorities. It wasn't the quotas that were laid on; it was finding that you really did get ideas that you wouldn't have come up in any other way, from a diverse team—and when I say diverse, I also mean internationally and culturally diverse. Some of our best ideas came from people in dramatically different cultures. Our people and our core values are the great differentiator. Our success comes from the integration of these principles married to some of the most capable talent in the world."

28 ──────────────

Jim Hackett

On September 11, 2001, the United States suffered terrorist attacks that cost nearly 3,000 lives and plunged the country into a defining change. The Pentagon, U.S. Department of Defense's headquarters, was attacked but not destroyed. A value-centered leader named Jim Hackett, formerly of Procter & Gamble (P&G) and now CEO of Steelcase, had made a decision months earlier that proved core values are strategic and may, in fact, save lives.

"At Steelcase," he says, "we make office furniture, as well as other product solutions for the workplace. One such product is a movable wall that you might see in a cubicle. During observational research, we began playing with the height of these walls. You could buy a wall that was only five feet tall, or one that went all the way to the ceiling. The wall frames were then covered with removable panels, or skins. Products like these allowed a company to make their space as flexible as possible. They can simply take off all the skins, reconfigure the shape of the space, and put the skeleton back together—reapplying the skins without regard to the height they used to be. The genius in the design was the underlying geometry, so everything would fit regardless of how the user wanted to arrange it. It was a pretty innovative idea."

"We later found out that there are different fire codes for those surfaces. It makes sense when you think about it, because when fire codes were first invented for commercial buildings, there was no such thing as a cubicle. So the cubicle, when it came to be, actually had more strict standards for fire retention or suppression than the full-height wall. Because we had designed only one standard for this product, we knew that it was very likely that it would be used out of standard depending on where the customer put it. "This led us to recall something close to $50 million worth of product," he said. "I went to our board and their question was, 'Why are we doing this? We haven't had a complaint. There have been no fires.' I explained that our customers bought this from us thinking that Steelcase stands for integrity. 'What did our competitors do?' they asked. I said, 'Many of them don't meet the fire codes today.' I believed that the culture of Steelcase was to do the right thing. We recalled the product and replaced it. It was very difficult, because it financially affected employees and top management across the board. It was a very palpable moment."

"So, a few weeks go by," he says. "We'd finished one of the renovation wings of the Pentagon, and the next day, the attacks of 9/11 happened and the plane hit the side of the building. If you ever look at those pictures, you'll see that the windows to the right and left of the impact aren't even cracked. It's because the Pentagon had been bolstered, made bomb proof, even though they never imagined a plane being used as a missile. From the external perspective, they actually had built a higher-than-standard facility. And inside, much of the furniture was product that we had replaced with the highest fire code standards in the world. That night I went to bed thinking that because the company had done the right thing, there may be those who survived based on the performance of our product."

"As CEO, you see those moments come back in a circle. Either you did the right thing, and there's actually a fundamental reward for that, or there's an acknowledgment that you did the wrong thing. The obstacles are significant because you have to deal with rationalization. They may say, 'We haven't heard there's a problem.' But it's still not the right thing."

"Somebody in the company said to me during this time, 'You know, Jim, everything burns.' My response was, 'Yes, and if your daughter was in that room, you would hope that the company that built all this stuff thought as strictly as I am about making sure that it didn't burn very easily or quickly.' We had to do a lot of things to recall the product, and yet there was something good that came out of it, and I'm confident more than ever that it was the right decision. Ken Blanchard once said, 'There's no softer pillow than a clear conscience.' That's a sentiment I completely related to at the time."

Where do core values originate, and how are they activated within a company to create a culture? "My perspective is that one of the strongest virtues of my time at P&G was how value-centered it was. The evidence of that was the way we actually assessed and recruited people; looking deeply for an intersection within a matrix of performance on one axis and values on the other. Reaching for the high end of both of those—high values and high performance—is no easy feat. If you had someone with strong performance characteristics, but there was a shady perspective on values, the belief was you would ultimately get in trouble. You had to confront that. Throughout the company, there was always a sense that we could find a solution—and do it with integrity. It's a never-say-die kind of perspective. At P&G, it was never over—you would find a way."

"My era with the company is 1977 to 1981, and even then P&G was ahead of its time. They began thinking very deeply about the nature of diversity that would carry the company into its future. Programs were incorporated to help broaden our sense of diversity. One area, for example, was learning more about the role of women. When I was a Sales Leader, it was called 'Women in Sales.' I had the pleasure to work with many remarkable and competent women. One particular day, I was chatting with a woman who worked for me, a highly regarded recruit out of DePauw University in Indiana. She came into my office one day and said, 'They are studying us?' You know, with a question mark. I loved that, because she was the kind of person that P&G wanted, someone who would be even indignant that there was a view of a difference. I said, 'No, it's because the men who are leaders needed to understand that most of the ways we practiced things weren't inclusive.' In the case of the role of women at P&G, there was a lot more to diversity than their being women, but it really started there. I have heard A.G. Lafley say that one of the core tenants of the company was its ability to market to women and also understand chemistry, so he simply narrowed it down to that, 'Women and chemistry.'"

"I remember going through a kind of enculturation of being around more women in the workplace during this time. Growing up with all brothers, it made a huge impact on me, and it's something that I still use today in leading people in my company."

"The nature of integrity within the company was a notion of whether someone was comfortable or not. I remember the first time I heard it from a colleague who said, 'I'm not comfortable with that.' The context of it was that we are now going into a space that we don't want to be in—an area that is unsettling to my inner being. I gained the utility of that understanding. In my leader role now, I notice people getting into trouble when they don't realize that, because we're human, we're bound to get near issues that border on questionable, and that ultimately challenge personal values. At P&G, this notion of whether you were comfortable meant it was okay for you to say no. It gave you permission to say no to doing the wrong thing."

Steelcase has kept its core values and principles at the center of the company. "At Steelcase, we feel our core values are a strategic point of difference. As leaders in office environment interior architecture, furniture, and technology, our market leadership strengths are bolstered by our own core values of acting with integrity, keeping commitments, telling the truth, treating people with dignity and respect, promoting positive relationships, and protecting the environment."

"We've added several transforming values at Steelcase, including 'know your business.' The essence of this was exhibited when I was with A.G. Lafley. We were walking down the hallway, and he turned to a passerby, and he said, 'So what's the penetration of Prilosec in the southeast?' He got an immediate clear answer. At P&G, it was expected that you would know the state of your business, because it was such a performance culture. I've adopted this mentality with my team at Steelcase. I feel we all need to be carrying this in our mind in a constant way so we're actually exchanging real information that helps the whole company perform better."

"One of those galvanizing moments in my career at P&G that forever changed me was a conversation with my boss John T. Ray, District Sales Manager of Case Foods, in Detroit. We were having dinner and, in explaining my tendency to think abstractly, I said to him that I find it to be a challenge when my brain seems to be moving independently of my mouth. I held him in super high regard and felt this was something he had achieved control of, so I asked if he could tell me what technique he used. He was frank and honestly said, 'I struggle with it.' I said, 'You're kidding me. You've mastered it.' He said, 'Not really. In fact, I felt the way you do when I started, because when I was young I was also inexperienced. What I decided is to put myself in more situations that are demanding of that, because the only way I was going to learn was by doing it over and over again.' When you run a company, when you're the CEO, you put yourself in situations often that you learn from, and sometimes these are situations that you don't particularly enjoy. That P&G moment was what it's all about—that's how you grow. I reflect back on that often."

"John T. Ray also taught me the core value of 'the candle of time' by involving me in Little League baseball as a coach. He drew me away from work and engendered lifelong principles through this experience. John wanted to know what his team members were doing for the community. He would put you in uncomfortable places because it was all about growing and learning. You had your work, your family, and your community. At P&G, they were not asking if you *wanted* to be involved in the community; it was a question of *how* you would involved. I've taken the liberty to adopt this practice at Steelcase and have expanded it to add a focus on health and well-being. I encourage my team to design their life to stay healthy. These leader jobs are very demanding and very difficult...Eating right, sleeping, and getting physical exercise are three things that I ask people about in their performance reviews. There's no food journal critique, record of miles run, or weigh-in at review time, but I want to know that they are making these areas a priority for their life. One of my employees said, 'Jim, I'll never be skinny.' And I said, 'That's not the issue. It's not a vanity question; it's the matter of your health. You can weigh whatever you want. I just want to know if you're gorging on donuts or exercising properly and getting sleep. A little accountability never hurt anyone.' Of course, I'm half teasing them when I do this, but I tell them that it really matters about taking care of themselves, because of what's going to be demanded. I feel by adding a focus on well-being, I've added to the lesson I borrowed from Ray. It's about supporting your employees in all facets of their lives."

For Jim Hackett, every aspect of business starts and ends with core values. His tomorrow will bring improvement to surrounding communities, movement to a sustainable future, encouragement of cultural awareness, and acceptance, all operating with values as their backbone.

29

Jose Luis Quintero

This is how deeply Jose Luis Quintero wove into his life the values he learned during his career with Procter & Gamble (P&G): They drove him to leave the company. After more than 20 years' service, spanning the divergent specialties of manufacturing and human resources leadership, in which he was posted to three other countries, his next assignment was to another overseas one. But personal circumstances demanded that he remain in his native Mexico. "What I am most grateful for about the years that P&G gave me was the opportunity to learn the importance of values and, many times," he says, "having to make an unpopular, even controversial decision for the sake of doing the right thing." While he had enjoyed his P&G career, he knew what he needed to do. So he quit. Although he left the company, he carried with him lessons about principles and foundations that he now shares as a life and business coach centered on being true to oneself.

Through his unique blending of production and personnel insights, he has conducted research that underscores the importance of clear priorities and values for effective leadership. He has distilled the lessons in two books: *Speed & Course* and *The Law of Your Reasons*, which offer a road map for finding one's life purpose and staying on track toward it. "Business savvy and entrepreneurial expertise on their own are not enough," he says. Leaders need to have a clear code of virtue-based personal conduct from which all else flows, he says, "We need to do the right things for the right reasons in order to get positive results."

173

Quintero recalls a client who ran a family-owned textile company. With his coaching, the woman who ran the business began to see double-digit growth from its rugs and tablecloths. But after a couple of years, she started to feel ashamed for no apparent reason. Things fell apart when a major department store requested an unusually large shipment. Her intuition told her not to, but she immediately purchased materials only usable for that specific client, who backed out on the deal only two days later, effectively leaving the business owner bankrupt. Quintero saw that the woman had veered from her personal code of conduct by trying to neutralize her shame by taking unnecessary risks with her business. "It was the virtues of dignity and identity she had drifted away from," he says. "I told her I would help her in negotiating with this client as long as she agreed to first correct her reasons." Reluctantly, the woman went back to her employees and the family and admitted she had made a terrible mistake by letting shame rule her decisions. "Two days later, this big department store company called her up and asked her to restart the deal because they really needed the product urgently," Quintero remembers. "She couldn't believe that going back to her own essential reasons could have such a powerful effect on what was going on in the outside world," he adds. "Now she is running a very successful business and also teaching this theory to many other women who have either started businesses or are already starting businesses throughout Mexico...that it's not only our actions that count; it's the reasons behind our actions, which are also critical to the outcome of our behavior."

Quintero's advice to the woman came from hard-won personal experience in his P&G days. After eight successful years with P&G in Mexico, he was offered one of the company's first international assignments from Latin America to the United States, running its Phoenix, Arizona, plant. Although the operation was less demanding than his previous responsibilities, "the results went south immediately." Quintero did what he knew how to do: work harder and longer. Six months later, things were no better, and he recalls being sunk in a depression so deep, he couldn't even answer e-mails. He thought he was either going to be fired or be sent back to Latin America with a lot of shame and having closed the doors for future Latin American managers in the U.S.

Quintero flew to Cancun to talk with his father, a successful businessman in his own right. His father asked whether his son was doing his best and how he had been selected for the position. Quintero said P&G made staffing choices mostly based on experience and performance records. So his father said, 'Well, you must be the best-prepared individual for such challenges then. If you're doing your best, applying your knowledge, and you're the best-prepared individual for the job—and you're still not delivering, that's not your problem.'" Quintero was not reassured. He could see only firing, shame, and failure. "Think about it," responded his father. "What else can you do? Doing better than your best? No. Can you apply knowledge you still don't have? Absolutely not. And replacing you with a less-prepared individual is a pretty poor choice too. So keep on doing your job, doing your best. Keep it up."

Quintero agreed that it seemed to make sense. "So I went back to Phoenix and, during the weekend, I decided that I would be okay just doing my best, enjoying my job, teaching my employees, and learning from them, regardless of whether the results were delivered or not."

When he walked back into the plant the next Monday morning, "it was a different reality. Everybody was cheerful, everybody was supporting my strategies. It started to improve at a pace I could not believe, and I did nothing different during that week—absolutely nothing different. The only thing difference was inside of me; I went back to my right reasons." Quintero realizes that he had rediscovered the way he had approached work back in his successful times in Mexico City. "I was enjoying it, learning, and sharing whatever knowledge I could share." He had tapped into his passions. The result: The Phoenix operation turned around, and when Quintero left for his next assignment in Venezuela, it was having achieved, not failed. "I had to accept that actions and effort [are] not all," he says of the experience. "Of course, we need to deliver effort. We need to do the right thing. But we also need to do the right things for the right reasons."

"I believe that Procter & Gamble exists for the right reasons. I believe it's a company with the right values, and its operating principles are just the best I've seen anywhere in any other company, either here or in any other country that I consult through my firm. That's what I am most grateful to P&G—values and principles. If we...not only do the right thing but do it for the right reason, it will pay out." He sees that it is possible to drift from core values for what seem at first blush to be legitimate reasons. In his case during the Phoenix struggles, he recognizes factors like success, recognition, making his father proud, providing new opportunities for his family, and opening the door for other Latinos. "All of these are honorable, but they shouldn't be the reasons—they should be the consequences of acting based on the right reasons."

Through his subsequent study, Quintero has come to believe that each person is motivated and inspired in his or her life by typically around 8 of some 28 virtues or values, such as dignity, forgiveness, loyalty, perseverance, patience, and tolerance. Like DNA, one individual's configuration and balance of these inner drivers will be different to everyone else's, but when someone identifies them and makes decisions and choices based on them, "absolutely marvelous things start happening in our lives."

Looking back, Quintero sees the principle in play through his troubled time in Phoenix. Having identified one of his eight core motivators as freedom, he now recognizes "as long as I felt free to work for P&G, my results were remarkable. The moment I moved to Phoenix—where I had a working visa that allowed me only to work as a manufacturing manager for that specific plant in that specific city—my freedom collapsed. Or, I allowed my freedom to collapse, to say it correctly." Quintero says that he let fear, shame, blame, regret, and worry become his impetus for action. "I thought I had made a mistake taking that assignment; I was feeling guilty. I wanted to prove to others that I could deliver. We're taught that there's nothing wrong with that, but there is—because the more we seek approval, the less we get it. The most reliable ways to obtain approval from others is to stop seeking it and acting for the right reasons."

He now sees that "when I was living in Mexico City, I could quit P&G any day and get another job. That made the results in P&G the best I could have, and it made me want to stay at P&G. The moment I declared that I was taking my freedom back in Phoenix, when I was delivering no results at all, and that I would enjoy my job regardless of the results, I was free again—and then the results started improving."

Doing the right thing can mean challenging conventional wisdom, however. Quintero recounts a time when labor negotiations in one Latin American country were bogged down. Both sides had followed the traditional maneuvers, in which the company would start by offering little or nothing and the unions would demand much more than they were really expecting.

Things were "very conflictive, very confrontational"—indeed P&G was close to pulling the plug on the operation and just walking away. Quintero decided to try to break the deadlock by offering to pay workers the raise the company had on offer ahead of any formal agreement. The move "violated every practice, but it was still the right thing to do for the right reasons," he admits. But "the employees were so grateful, were so trustful about this strategy we were sharing with them—because we also kept them well informed—that the next time we needed to increase salaries, the negotiation was very fluid, very positive...After that we had one of the best labor situations that I had the chance to work with." Within a few years, the once-fractious part of P&G was one of its most high-performing operations in Latin America, and Quintero was asked to summarize his actions in a report that became a blueprint for future labor negotiations in the company.

One reason that many organizations don't take the sort of radical steps Quintero advocates, though, is that they allow themselves to be dictated to by negative, rather than positive, pressures, "being too concerned about how it looks, not only what we do, but how what we do looks to others. "Sometimes we do have to make very controversial decisions. We need to act on them because we know it's the right thing." With that in mind, Quintero applauds P&G's clearly defined decision-making process, which involves weighing and evaluating all the evidence. "To me it says if a decision is made on time with the right involvement, with the right information and following the company's principles, it's a good decision—regardless of how it turns out. If it turns out well, good; if it turns out bad, good too—because we couldn't make a better decision than what we did. Sometimes fear of the decision not turning out well paralyzes organizations. But we can't run away from making decisions, because procrastinating is also making a decision."

The courage and clarity for making those hard calls needs to flow from the top, Quintero insists. In his consulting, "the first thing I do is make sure that the ultimate decision maker—the President or the owner or the General Manager—has a clear code of conduct and he or she follows that the best he or she can." As long as they do so, "then there is a chance for the company to keep growing at a constant speed and with a very clear course."

30

Samih Sherif

Few people have had as much opportunity to see how Procter & Gamble (P&G) applies its famed, unwavering core values up close in exacting business environments as Samih Sherif.

Born in 1925 in Palestine, under the British Mandate, and holding an almost legendary status within the company, the former Group Vice President had a hand in virtually every distributorship, every joint venture, every new brand introduction, and new market opening from Chile to China over the 31 years of his career. As long-time leader of the Export and Special Operations Division (E&SO), headquartered in Geneva, Switzerland, Sherif not only pioneered the rapid globalization of the company's business into new markets in Asia and the Far East, but continued to pursue the profitable growth of its core business in the Middle East. The region's cultural and traditional attitudes intersecting deal-making could be at odds, especially with P&G's no-nonsense approach to business—a potential clash Sherif was aware of before even joining the company.

He was working for a commercial radio station that P&G used extensively to advertise Tide to the Pan-Arab audience, and he got to know several P&G managers who were handling the company's Middle East business. "I was impressed by their ability and their straightforwardness," he recalls. They were "candid, honest, and fair. They were people of character, with a congenial approach." When Sherif was approached about joining the organization, he was impressed by "their comprehension of the unorthodox ways and means of doing business in the Arab World and what it would take to do it the P&G

way. We were clearly on the same wavelength, concerning our insights and fundamental principles." Those core values and principles were ones that Sherif held to in personal as well as professional life: "Honesty, candor, fairness, mutual respect, and a collective determination to achieve goals."

Holding to those ideals could be demanding. Sherif recalls getting a call one time from the manager of a Packaged Soap and Detergent plant in a part of the region experiencing great internal strife and friction. The Plant Manager told him that the head of a group claiming to be a security unit wanted to talk to him personally. "I asked if he knew what the guy wanted," Sherif recounts. "He said, 'Probably money.'" When the other man came on the line, he shared a long story of how he and a group of armed men from the region took on the task of protecting inhabitants, shop owners, and industrial buildings like P&G's from attacks by bandits. "I said, 'That's fine, but are you part of the government security forces?' He said, 'The government is dysfunctional. We are doing the job, and we hope you will take good care of us. Otherwise, there will be serious consequences.'" Sherif said, "Listen carefully to what I am going to tell you. First, we do not pay bribes. Second, we did not ask you to protect our plant. We do not pay for a service we did not require. If the serious consequence of not paying you is that you will ransack or blow up the plant—just forewarn the workers to leave the building and blow it up if you dare." And with that, Sherif hung up the phone. He picked it up again quickly, to call his boss at P&G Cincinnati headquarters and tell him what had happened. "I took a risky decision," Sherif admits. But the plant was not touched.

That encounter summed up Sherif's approach. "Wherever we did business, we adhered to the company's values," he says. "No compromise. When values and interests didn't coincide, we held onto our values and sacrificed the interests."

Another situation that called for a tough stance occurred in South Korea in the mid-1980s. Following successful negotiations with a well-established company in the country, P&G was on the verge of signing a partnership agreement. But on the eve of the deal's closure, the South Korean Chairman raised questions about the technical assistance fees due to P&G and how they could be remitted. This issue had been dealt with at length during the negotiations. For P&G, one of the key provisions in the joint venture was its right to recover foreign costs like R&D and allocated overheads before splitting local profit.

"We believed that our prospective partners agreed with our position," Sherif remembers. "We counted on their support to get the government's approval to remit the fees to P&G in hard currency." But the Chairman's last-minute questioning made Sherif and his colleagues suspect that he was not truly supportive of P&G's position and that he might actually hinder the government approval to serve his company's interests. "With no trust, there can be no deal," Sherif says. "Our reaction was quick and firm. We told him the deal was off."

The decision cost P&G expansion—for the time being. Several years later, after Sherif's retirement, he learned that P&G had secured a joint venture agreement in South Korea with a different company. For Sherif, that illustrates why P&G's values have stood the test of time. "Simply because honest people, be they entrepreneurs or companies, can succeed in business if they hold on to their fundamental values and principles and speak out without equivocation," he says.

Good management is a moral undertaking, Sherif asserts. "Of course, the bottom line is a key objective, but the way to get it with honesty is fundamental for the long-term viability of an enterprise." Such an approach requires ruthless self-examination, as well as critical evaluation of others. Recognizing that the E&SO operated in countries "where bribery was simply an exchange of favors, we needed to remain aware of the temptation and risk" at home. That meant regular monitoring of P&G operations, with personal contact "at all levels of the organization—from the CEO down to country managers." In addition, there would be formal internal audits. "I would brief the internal auditor before his missions and ask him to be extra-alert to transactions with third parties that involved middle and lower management," Sherif recalls. "We actually discovered a couple of instances where there were kickbacks on printing Tide packages in a North African market. We made that public, and the guy was instantly fired. That kind of unflinching commitment to doing the right thing internally in turn made it easier to require the same standards of others. In the case of joint ventures and large distribution organizations, it was critical to tell prospective partners what values we held and our expectation that they would abide by them with no reservation," Sherif says.

"If we lost our trust, we had provisions in our contracts to terminate, walk away, or buy back their shareholding. But, apart from the South Korean case, we experienced no conflict in the domain of values." Reflecting on the essentials he embraced during his P&G career, Sherif says: "All good (and bad) values are learned and taught by example. P&G is a rock-solid company that attends to details. Although it is seen by some employees as an uptight management, it is, in fact, a process of thoroughness that is pivotal for success. A self-developing organization is best for keeping superior people who have instinctive feel for the business and a deep sense of ownership. They are the potential future leaders."

31

Bob Herbold

In his most recent book titled *What's Holding You Back?*, Bob Herbold describes courageous leadership as a fine blend of insight, instinct, and decisiveness: the willingness and ability to follow the facts wherever they may lead. You must also realize that you often can't get all the data you need, there are often multiple options, and each has pluses and minuses, yet you need to make a decision and get on with things. That delicate balance is the distillation of his wisdom gleaned from the vantage point of almost four decades' leadership with two iconic businesses: Procter & Gamble (P&G) and Microsoft.

Describing the leadership insights he now shares through his own consultancy group as "almost 40 years of battle scars," Herbold is the author of three leadership books. He tackles topics such as the devastating nature of silos and fiefdoms and how to deal with them, the ravages of success and how it seduces leaders to be excessively proud and lose their sense of urgency, and the importance of guts and courage in dealing with tough decisions and leading an organization.

Too often managers shy away from tough decisions because there is no "right" answer. A decision needs to be made, and you need to trust yourself. In these situations, managers too often rely on teams, task forces, and consensus. Herbold challenges the strong emphasis placed on teams these days. While there is a time and a place for "input from lots of angles," he says, "when you're looking for innovation or creativity or are driving important change, consensus is the kiss of death. The way to destroy an innovative idea or a significant change is to expose it to a consensus process or a committee. The reason is

183

everybody will chip away at it and take all the unique aspects away, thus making it average and acceptable to everyone. Your significant change will become a modest step forward at best. Your innovative new product idea will become a modest improvement at best, and such things don't sell much in the marketplace. Innovative, exciting things sell. So be careful where you're using consensus."

A former Senior Vice President with P&G before helping lead software giant Microsoft through one of its biggest growth periods, serving as Chief Operating Officer, Herbold finds the essence of great business to be pretty uncomplicated. Pointing to P&G as a prime example, he observes: "This company is totally focused on the consumer. The trick is to get bright ideas that excite consumers more than your competitor's offerings, and then executing well and winning in the marketplace. It's that simple." But simple does not necessarily mean easy. That's because once people have achieved a level of success or stability, they tend to want to play it safe and keep things the way they are rather than innovate or change. "Once people are in a job for a while and feeling stable, unfortunately, the human brain is wired in such a way that it is looking for ways to keep that stability," Herbold says, "and it tends to work hard to blunt the impact of any new ideas that might require change."

Herbold points out one other common problem managers have: "They hire too many people, causing the organization to get more and more complicated, adding layers of management, too many projects, excessive systems, and bureaucratic procedures. Pretty soon it's hard to do work, and people spend a high percentage of their time going to meetings and sending e-mails...."

The subject of being objective and open to change is a topic Herbold pushes hard. One of his heroes in this area is John Smale, a very successful P&G CEO in the 1980s. In 1979, when Herbold was a Brand Assistant on Sure deodorant, colleagues in the Crest brand group pitched a radical suggestion for Crest toothpaste. Rival Unilever's Aim had arrived on the scene with a kids' toothpaste, successfully positioned as offering a flavor kids would love so much they would no longer fight brushing, and, in fact, would brush longer. This would solve mom's problem of getting the kid to brush. Members of the Crest brand put together a memo, including consumer research on a new Crest kid's flavor that P&G R&D had developed, that proposed the launch of a test market of a kids' flavored line extension of Crest. It flew in the face of the brand's long-time positioning focused on the value of cavity protection—seen as a weightier testimony than a nice taste. The proposal went all the way up through the ranks with total support and was finally forwarded to Ed Harness, the CEO in the late 1970s. After a few weeks, he sent it back down to the brand group with just one handwritten note on the cover page: "Please suspend this until I retire." The brand group learned that his issue was that he believed a kids' flavor on Crest flew in the face of the brand's hugely successful cavity protection strategy. Those on the brand group who had pushed the idea "all felt scolded," Herbold recalls. A year later, in 1980, Herbold found himself on the Crest brand group as Assistant Brand Manager. About that same time, CEO Ed Harness retired. Equally important, Aim with its kids' flavor continued to grow. The new CEO at P&G was John Smale—the man widely recognized as the father of Crest, since he was the Crest Brand Manager when Crest got the American Dental Association seal of approval.

Herbold noted that, in 1980, further research persuaded those on the Crest brand group that the company should revisit the children's product idea, but they were at the same time "somewhat reluctant to put their career on the line and float this up." But the brand group decided to propose the test market of a kids' flavor on Crest once again. When he received the proposal, Smale was intrigued. He asked for more consumer testing. In particular, he asked that consumer research be done that measured the reputation of Crest regarding cavity protection after extended use of the kids' flavor of Crest. Herbold says, "The thing that impressed me at that juncture was John Smale's reasonableness in looking at the consumer data very hard and trying to be objective and open minded, even though you knew that this is a man who put his life into Crest and was the father of cavity protection in the toothpaste business." Herbold was impressed that here was someone who was "not a victim of his past. He was willing to put aside yesterday's business model." As a result, P&G launched a test market and then successfully expanded nationally a kids'-flavored Crest line extension, slowing Aim's march and then causing the start of its downward spiral that was never reversed.

Seduced by Success, one of three leadership and management books Herbold has written since leaving Microsoft, looks more deeply at the issue exemplified by the Crest challenge. "The lesson is be objective; don't be afraid to change your business model," he says. "In fact, you're going to get run over if you don't consider changing your business model all the time. Watch your competitors, and don't think for a moment that since you had success in the past...you're going to be successful in the future. That was a core lesson that I learned very early from that Crest project, and John Smale was the epitome of this thinking."

Looking to avoid rocking the boat leads to another threat to businesses and organizations: the fortress mentality. Herbold explored this in his first book, *The Fiefdom Syndrome*. He believes managers have an innate tendency to "start building a moat around their organization, so that when change comes, it affects other people and not them. They just want to be left alone and focus on protecting their turf." He has an answer: "You have to reorganize regularly, so people don't get stuck." After a year or so in a new job, people typically start to feel more comfortable in their abilities. "Right at that stage, you are starting to go downward in your ability to deal with fresh ideas and change," he says. "One of the most powerful tools in terms of fighting off the fiefdom syndrome is to move people around and reconfigure the organization. Also, you need to spot those people who are uniquely capable of dealing with change and are really change agents, and you put those people in the jobs that need that kind of thinking the most."

Some fields lend themselves more naturally to change. Herbold found that out for himself when he left P&G, the epitome of a measured, considered approach to new products, for Microsoft, where the speed of technological change demanded faster action. Herbold had no plans to depart from P&G. But with a PhD in computer science and being a self-confessed "sucker for technology," the offer to join Bill Gates' company as executive vice president and chief operating officer in 1994, as testing was going full bore of its forthcoming Windows 95, was "too much fun to pass up." Due to be launched the following year, the operating system was a quantum leap forward from the company's existing offering.

The computer world may have required the same kind of deliberate data for decision making that the consumer products world looked for—more so, if anything—but there was no time for carefully created proposals. "Speed: that was a big difference," Herbold says. "No memos, because you didn't have time for that. You just went next door and twisted Bill's arm with as many facts as you could, but with no time to write anything." Though it was in some ways a coming home to his original discipline for Herbold, he arrived at Microsoft following 26 years at P&G where he started in Industrial Engineering and R&D, but he ended up spending most of his time in Marketing. Upon arriving at Microsoft, he soon realized that the company may have been a software giant, but no one there "really cared much or knew much about consumer marketing." Herbold was also dealing with a boss notoriously cautious about spending money, especially in an area as foreign to the precision required for software development as advertising. But the new Windows 95 product cried out for an emphatic launch that would make people sit up and take notice. Herbold knew that he had his work cut out in presenting to Gates the marketing proposal that was developed for Windows 95, even though he was sure that advertising agency Widen & Kennedy's campaign—unveiling the new operating system (OS) to the insistent drive of the Rolling Stones' lurching "Start Me Up"—was a hit. With the idea scoring high in testing, Herbold took the proposal to Gates, who liked what he saw. As Herbold puts it, "And I said, 'Now, are you ready for the bad news? It will cost us $3 million just to get the rights to the song. Plus, you know, we want to spend about maybe $80 to $100 million on air time.' And he about fell out of his chair."

Undeterred, Herbold asked to screen the ad the following day for around 30 of Microsoft's key leaders, with Gates present. "Those folks went nuts; they were euphoric," Herbold recalls. "So I went back to Bill and said, 'We have to spend this money. It's a fabulous investment in the future.'" Gates remained unpersuaded but said he would think about it some more. Meanwhile, Herbold went back to his team, needing to nail down projected sales. "We made some very conservative estimates based on consumer research (the P&G way), which showed the percent of people who claimed strong interest in the product. We went back and argued some more, and finally, convinced him. Gates' conclusion was 'Okay, you're crazy, but I'll let you do it because it's a once-in-a-lifetime deal.'" The rock and roll-out was "a smashing hit," Herbold says. "You remember the news stories, of people lining up at midnight to buy this operating system. It was a sensational hit...I don't think there's ever been a bigger marketing event in the category."

For Herbold, his P&G schooling is woven throughout the Windows 95 experience. As he looks back: "You see a lot of Procter principles in action: getting the data on product performance, doing research on consumer interest, waiting around for the really big idea form the ad agency, and then pouring the coals to it and making the big bets. This is a classic example." It also underscores the importance of making bold moves. "You need something significant that ideally is a game changer for your industry," Herbold says. "In other words, you need big ideas, and people who simply live in the world of numerous low-impact projects don't understand that, and they waste a lot of time. People get so tied up doing so many things and get so busy when what they should do is kill most of those small ideas and work to find and exploit the big one."

The lesson in the power of focus relates to another aspect of the Windows 95 launch. Although some observers criticize Microsoft for having missed the significance of the coming Internet in the mid-90s, Herbold tells how the company actually was well aware of the potential of an online world as it focused singlemindedly on the Windows 95 launch. In early 1995, while Microsoft was totally immersed in the preparation of Windows 95, one of the recently hired computer science wizards showed senior company leaders a web browser developed at the University of Illinois that was now being refined at a start-up company called Netscape. For these execs, it was "really the first serious encounter with the Internet." The question was: What to do? The answer: Nothing. Gates pointed to the August 24, 1995 launch date for Windows 95 and announced that the company would not give focused attention to the Internet before that. Then, in the late afternoon of Windows 95 launch day when all the festivities were complete, Herbold remembers, "we all met in Bill's office, saying, 'Okay, now how are we going to take advantage of the Internet?'"

Herbold was "impressed" with Gates' gutsy decision. Here was a superb businessman making a priority decision to do a big thing, namely Windows 95, really, really well. He put the right priorities on things. "It was a huge lesson for me in terms of the value of a nervy decision to do the big things with real care and to put aside and not get distracted. You meet people who are working on seven things; you go in, they're just totally disorganized. They're going to meetings all the time, acting important—and then they get nothing done of significance. So (Gates' leadership) was a powerful lesson."

Herbold says, "The examples of objectivity and open-mindedness at P&G and the focus and excellence at Microsoft strongly suggest that great companies are built first and foremost on values. The enterprises' ability to live out these core values accelerates company performance and gives each employee the essential ground rules. Armed with the core values and leadership principles, nothing should hold a company back."

Part VI
Changing Lives

32

Charlotte Otto

Over the years, many have asked why a marketing powerhouse like P&G hasn't done more to build what is arguably its biggest, oldest brand: Procter & Gamble. This question has been debated for decades. The answer has changed over time, reflecting P&G's remarkable ability to evolve while holding its core values constant...and the answer is still evolving.

Ed Artzt called the question after becoming Chief Executive in 1990 when he proclaimed, "P&G will stand visibly behind its brands." The responsibility for bringing this challenge to life fell to Bob Wehling, P&G Senior Vice President of Public Affairs, and Charlotte Otto, who then led Public Relations. "Ed saw the importance of building the familiarity and reputation of the company *behind* P&G brands," Otto recalls. "He understood the business value from his years of P&G International experience. He also understood rising expectations for corporate responsibility, particularly in the United States and Europe. It was no longer acceptable for big corporations to hide under the desk and hope nobody noticed."

Ed's vision challenged more than a century of thinking that "building the corporate brand was not only unnecessary, it could be downright dangerous. Many argued that if the brands and P&G were visibly linked, a brand that got in trouble could bring the whole house down," Otto says. "Others pointed out that no consumer ever bought a Procter & Gamble—you couldn't find any Procter & Gambles on the shelf—so why would the company invest resources in something that consumers couldn't buy? There was a very strong belief, built up over many years, that the P&G brand should be invisible and silent."

Even with these long-held beliefs, there still was recognition that the P&G brand could—in limited situations—add value. Otto observes, "Brands could use 'New from Procter & Gamble' for six months, and then it had to come off the package. The rules were strictly enforced. While the use of the Procter & Gamble 'brand' was rare, it was purposeful."

Otto well knows the importance of the Procter & Gamble name through her years as P&G's Global External Relations Officer. The company's first female corporate officer, she oversaw an international team responsible for public relations, employee and shareholder communications, consumer relations, and liaison with governments and other stakeholders.

"External Relations' role is to build and protect the business and reputation of P&G and its brands," she says. "In essence, we are the company storytellers. It's all about understanding and building relationships, and then finding ways to tell the company story that engages people, that's credible, and invites them to care."

In 1990, Artzt's foresight was based on direct business value. "We could see that a significant proportion of P&G growth would be coming from geographic expansion into countries where neither our company nor our brands were known," Artzt recently observed. "This was particularly important in Japan where consumer loyalty to companies was a major factor in brand selection. In China and Russia, where people had been using government-made brands of poor quality, consumers were skeptical of any new foreign products from companies they knew nothing about. It was not a one-shot effort, but a continuing requirement for success."

Under Artzt's leadership, P&G's external profile increased markedly. Yet, corporate efforts to build the P&G brand were slowed by the Gulf War and other issues. Some P&G leaders outside the United

States cautioned that it could be counterproductive by needlessly raising the profile of a U.S.-based company. Nonetheless, efforts to establish the P&G brand continued, particularly in developing geographies.

John Pepper, who followed Artzt as CEO, encouraged the P&G brand team to establish Procter & Gamble as the consumers' indispensible partner by offering advice and usage ideas to build a bond with users. Consumer Relations could be a key part in bringing this to life. Pepper understood that building the P&G brand wasn't about corporate advertising—it was about *actions*, driven by P&G's Purpose, Values, and Principles. Being, and being seen as, the consumer's ally was at the heart of this. However, it ultimately became difficult to scale this approach.

Pepper's successor, Durk Jager, also was a strong supporter of building the P&G brand. In 1999, the team launched an internal P&G brand campaign with the tag line "Imagine What's Next." This captured Jager's strong focus on innovation to drive growth. But after the stock crash in 2000, this slogan became a bad joke among employees and was dropped. The efforts to more systematically build the P&G brand did not come to fruition until A.G. Lafley's tenure.

Coming off several earnings warnings, a precipitous drop in stock price, and the resignation of CEO Durk Jager in 2000, there was an "enormous crisis of confidence among our employees," Otto remembers. "A.G. recognized right away that we were going to have to define again what the company stood for. Are our Purpose and Values still relevant? Are we still serious about them, and how do they come to life in this crisis situation?" Lafley believed that building the P&G brand could be part of the plan to rebuild confidence. But first things first; priority #1 was to get the business back on track.

About a year after becoming CEO, when the business started to improve, Lafley agreed to restart the P&G brand-building effort. "We needed to refocus people," Otto says. "A reinvigoration of the P&G Purpose and Values and P&G equity was essential."

Otto oversaw research to define what P&G stood for among employees in key countries. "The results were unremarkable, yet transformative. They told us things we already knew, yet the research articulated the company's essence more clearly than we could see, even though it was there right in front of us all along."

"In the minds of employees, P&G stood for leadership, for connecting with consumers, and for its core purpose of improving lives. Those simple ideas became the P&G brand equity statement: 'in touch, in the lead, improving lives.' These ideas were amazingly consistent around the world, and deeply grounded in P&G's Purpose and heritage."

Lafley already had begun to reinforce the constancy of P&G's Purpose and Values. "Beginning with his first 'world tour' after being named CEO, P&G values were at the center of his conversations," Otto recalls. "He also helped people understand that part of the reason the business was underperforming was that we had lost touch with consumers. To get the business back on track, A.G. focused people on 'Consumer Is Boss' and on being more in-touch with consumers, customers, competition, stakeholders, and each other. This created a business and behavioral mandate for developing the P&G brand story."

The P&G brand creative work was developed by the Saatchi & Saatchi account/creative team led by Tim Love and Dick Holt. Otto recalls, "When they presented the selling idea 'Touching Lives, Improving Life,' we knew they'd nailed it. This was an inspiring expression of the P&G brand equity. We loved it right away."

A small team, initially led by Kelly Brown and later by Diana Shaheen, then developed—for the first time—a true P&G-style branding program, including visual equity, audiences, and even brand advertising tags. The early "marketing plan" was primarily focused on employees and recruits, however. Lafley used it as a way to focus employees on being more in-touch.

Reflecting on the early research, Lafley comments, "A helpful piece of analysis for me was an assessment of which stakeholders might be more responsive to and influenced by the P&G brand promise. This led us to begin with employees, recruits, investors, customers, and supplier partners."

Shaheen was instrumental in defining the P&G "in-touch" experience and specific behaviors to ensure the brand equity translated into real actions that would help the business. "It was a big breakthrough when 'in-touch' was adopted as one of the 'Success Drivers,'" Otto observes. (The Success Drivers are an update of the traditional "What Counts Factors.") "This was the behavior that we most needed to dial-up to get the business back on track." It was clear to Otto that if "Touching Lives, Improving Life" had not been directly tied to the business and behaviors, it would not have been sustainable.

Lafley also recalls the emphasis on tying P&G brand-building to business goals. "Among the early stakeholder priorities were governments and regulatory bodies, and even NGOs. We were effective with governments from Beijing to Brussels to Washington, DC and beyond because we had built a strong P&G brand reputation and a track record for productive private/public partnerships."

"Even with strong CEO support, corporate initiatives—coming from the 'center' of the organization—often face skepticism from the business units as to why they are worth the effort," Otto says. "Certainly this was the case with P&G brand building over many years, but tying it to a business imperative helped it to take hold."

Otto is proud to have helped build the foundation of the P&G brand over the two decades since Artzt first declared that P&G would stand visibly behind its brands. Yet, during her tenure, the P&G brand was primarily leveraged internally, with recruits and with corporate stakeholders such as investors and business partners. There had not been any significant consumer-facing efforts, particularly in the United States.

This changed in 2010, after Otto's retirement. With the encouragement of new CEO Bob McDonald and Global Marketing Officer Marc Pritchard, P&G brand marketing efforts are moving to a new level.

Greg Icenhower, Director of Corporate Communications & Reputation, was a member of the original P&G brand team. Today, he is the global External Relations leader for the P&G Brand and offers some perspective on this evolution. He observes, "Bob brings a conviction about this work formed in large part by his experience in Asia. He came into the CEO job with a guiding belief in the power of competing as one company and communicating with one voice while enabling P&G product brands to coexist with one another and the company brand in a way others can't. This makes him the most passionate champion yet for building the P&G brand."

A true breakthrough came with P&G's "Proud Sponsor of Moms" campaign launched at the 2010 Winter Olympics. P&G became an Olympic sponsor in late 2009, so there wasn't much time to put a program together before the February 2010 games. As Pritchard describes it in remarks at the 2010 Cannes Advertising Festival, "We started with a traditional approach where 18 different brands sponsored athletes to support brand-specific programs. But that just didn't feel like it was enough. We challenged ourselves to come up with an idea that unites the Purpose of P&G with the purpose of the Olympics."

"At first glance, it wasn't obvious what P&G and 18 different brands had in common with the Olympic movement until we realized that every Olympic athlete has a mom who has supported them and sacrificed for them throughout their lives. P&G appreciates moms for all they do to support children every day. From this insight, we created an idea to express gratitude to moms everywhere through our 'P&G Proud Sponsor of Moms' idea." The program included a "Thank You Mom" gift to offset travel costs so that every U.S. athlete's mom could attend the games and see her child compete.

The program was supported by a multifaceted marketing program that for the first time included a major advertising program in the United States, linking P&G and its product brands. In Pritchard's words, "It gave consumers a view of what the people in P&G around the world care about."

The "Moms" campaign defied long-held principles about the primacy of product brands and proved that with the right idea—grounded in the company's Purpose—the P&G brand can provide the halo of a caring, generous, "in-touch" corporate parent.

The results were impressive. During the Games, the program delivered more than 8 billion impressions, P&G's favorability jumped 10 points, and sales increased over $100 million. This experience led to a remarkable 10-year global Olympics partnership. This is by far the company's largest sponsorship agreement and an indication of its deep commitment to building the P&G brand.

This Olympics campaign is an amazing leap in a P&G brand-building journey that started two decades earlier. "It's amazing to see Ed Artzt's 1990 articulation that 'P&G will stand visibly behind its brands' come fully to life in 2010," Otto observes. "The time became right (at last) to make the P&G brand more visible to consumers."

Otto has passed the baton to other P&G corporate storytellers, but remains a loyal and proud P&G brand champion. "It would have been easy to drop the P&G branding effort at several points along the road, but I'm glad we didn't," she said. "It ultimately was right for the business and certainly reflects P&G's ability to challenge accepted beliefs and evolve. It's one of the company's great keys to sustained success."

33

Mohan C. Mohan

More than a decade after retiring from Procter & Gamble (P&G) at the close of a successful career with the company, Mohan C. Mohan remains a card-carrying enthusiast for its values and foundations. Literally. His family teases him about his undying loyalty to the firm, but he doesn't waver. He makes sure that he always has a copy of P&G's value-driven mission statement with him, and he regularly refers to this both personally and professionally as he invests in the lives of tomorrow's business leaders. Serving as a volunteer advisor to business schools in Europe, the United States, and his homeland of India, Mohan unabashedly cites P&G as the well from which he draws to pass on advice and insights.

Fundamentally, he believes, successful business is not so much about having good plans as it is about developing good relationships, both within the organization and externally. It is that principle that leads to strong products and loyal customers. "It may initially take a bit longer, but it pays rich dividends," he says. "It's not rocket science, but when we are under pressure in our daily lives, we can sometimes forget the basics."

Mohan saw the importance of these two dimensions of building strong relationships in a wide-ranging series of assignments that took him to various countries in Europe, the Middle East, and Africa. Joining the company in 1972, he became known for his gift of opening new markets, ending his P&G time as General Manager/Vice President, Health and Beauty Care, UK/Ireland.

If there was a secret to his achievements, it was passed on by Herbert Schmitz, a boss he had in his younger years. "He saw me trying to figure out the best way to succeed and to make an impact. I will never forget what he told me," he recalls. "He said, 'Mohan, you need to do only three things: Promote the business, promote your team, and promote your boss. Then guess what's going to happen to you?'" Most importantly, that guidance centered on P&G's focus on aligning the objectives and interests of the company with those of the individual. "In other words, they measured your success as the company's success and the company success was viewed by the individual as their success. It was a core strategic value."

A natural outflow of that interconnectedness led to the conviction that if the company concentrated on doing what was best for its consumers, they in turn would reward the firm with their loyalty—and those customers' communities would prosper in turn. "Your objectives and the company's objectives are inseparable," Mohan says. "So, keep pushing the business; keep pushing your team, make them develop and grow; keep challenging your bosses, and speak nicely about them as they are there to help you grow. By doing this, you are leveraging the entire organization and therefore, despite your limitations, you are bound to succeed—of course, you must be determined and commit yourself to the firm for the long haul."

Mohan suggests a similar, three-chord weave to the thousands of business students he now mentors and encourages. He urges them to look for three things when they are deciding where they want to invest their time and talents. "One, what is the quality of people with whom you will be working? Two, what are the principles of that particular organization, and do you believe in them? Three, what is the organization's purpose?" If all three align, then sign up, he advises. "Go and work for them, whether that happens to be in consulting, consumer goods, manufacturing, investment banking, or private equity—it doesn't matter." The key is being enthusiastic about a firm's people, principles, and purpose. Enthusiasm and passion improve your chances of having a successful career and a fulfilling work-life balance. "Now, that does not mean that every day of the year and every hour of the day, you're going to be excited. There will be good days; there will be bad days. Consider another P&G principle. As long as 60% of your decisions are productive, you will succeed. Of course, you aim to make only great decisions, but be realistic; expect some mistakes."

Today, Mohan considers coaching others as payback for what he received as a young man. "I can't thank my first managers enough," he says. "Without even realizing it, they had a profound impact on both my life and my family's life." He points to his two daughters, one a surgeon in the United States, and the other working in financial services in the UK. "Even without my communicating these values to them explicitly, they have implemented them in their careers," he says. "I know it has had a lasting impact because, by any stretch of the imagination, they have been very successful."

Nurturing newcomers was an integral part of Mohan's successful strategy at P&G. Having explored new markets in the Middle East at the beginning of his career, in 1985 he was asked to go to Egypt. The country had presented numerous challenges to the company. "One of the biggest concerns was our ability to conduct honest business in the country. Several senior executives had visited, and they had serious concerns." But Mohan believed in the opportunity. He leveraged prior experience in this assignment. He hired people locally and developed this talent. "While building relationships with Egyptian-based universities, we began attracting young people, recruiting and training them. Once aboard, we instilled the basic principles of the company in them and continuously reinforced the key messages. Within our team, we rigidly implemented our strategies, nurturing professionals who embodied P&G core values." Applying what he experienced in Saudi Arabia where he was responsible for introducing Pampers to a country unfamiliar with the idea of disposable diapers, Mohan spent an inordinate amount of time transforming his people. He became the consummate mentor and coach to hundreds of professionals. "In fact, one of my bosses used to say in my feedback, 'You could work fewer hours if you were to spend less time being a teacher rather than a manager.' I said, 'No, I would rather teach people and develop them. Ultimately, this will benefit the business.'" A quarter century on, "the Egyptian business is extremely profitable. I continue to hear so many positive stories on how we have successfully expanded our business."

The unrelenting willingness to train others continues to fuel his work with students today. "You don't have to be Mother Teresa, Martin Luther King, or John F. Kennedy, but you can make an impact [that] will multiply over the longer term," he says. "In other words, it's like viral marketing. You don't have to be in a powerful position. Whatever you are, wherever you are, you can easily help everybody by taking away lessons from your experiences and passing them on to others." It was only later during his P&G tenure that Mohan learned the reason that he had been selected for many of his positions. The firm believed in his patience, his commitment in developing his people, and his unswerving commitment to ensuring alignment with the company's values. "Whatever I did, I would never do anything unethical, illegal, or immoral," he says. "My colleagues knew that I would not fall for any temptations in terms of bending the rules, breaking laws, or bribing in order to increase market share. I was focused on maintaining integrity at all costs. I strove to be a transformational manager rather than a transactional one."

Mohan says that the simplicity, but clarity of P&G's purpose—the commitment to doing the right thing for your customers and the right thing for your employees—can be underappreciated. "I'm not a scholar, but it appears to me that the reason we are currently experiencing difficult economic conditions is because we forgot why banks existed," he remarks. "Banks existed in the good old days as institutions to take care of people's money and to manage that money better than the individual could—which means they were responsible, they were caring, and they had an expertise. By 2000, banks were working as gamblers. They were lending money to people who didn't have the capability to repay. How did they forget their original job? Never would this happen in a company like P&G. The kind of people who work with P&G—it could not. In talking with people outside of P&G, I have learned that you can undervalue a company [that] focuses on its core values. It is essential that you use that knowledge so as to help people in a variety of walks of life." Looking in the rear view mirror, Mohan also sees that what was accepted as just commonplace at P&G is a rarity elsewhere. "There were times when I felt that the outside world was a lot better in conducting business than what we were. Often I felt we were too slow, too bureaucratic, and not feeding external ideas into the company."

The world has changed in many ways since Mohan arrived at P&G fresh out of Columbia University as a new Marketing Assistant in Ireland, but he thinks that it is easy to overcomplicate the issues of decision-making in today's fast-paced world. "It's very simple for me," he says. "Whether you have a camel, Volkswagen, or Ferrari pulling your cart, you want to go from point A to point B safely, quickly, and economically." Although technology means information needs to be gathered to make a decision as quickly as possible, actual decision-making times have not changed. Regardless of the speed of information, true leaders are called to do the right things with that information. And that core value can extend to doing it right the first time. That core value can also mean taking time to teach values to the next generation.

34 ———————————————————————

Harry Leibowitz

The lives of countless disadvantaged children around the world have been bettered through Harry Leibowitz's passion for helping others, a lifelong commitment shaped and refined in his years with Procter & Gamble (P&G). Although he arrived at the company with charitable effort an unquestioned part of his make-up, it was while he was there that he learned how to ask of others in a way that has multiplied giving and action almost immeasurably. The World of Children Awards he founded in 1998 has impacted the lives of more than 30 million children by funding innovative programs and, in telling their stories through the Nobel Prize-like honors bestowed, inspiring others to action, too.

Ironically, Leibowitz's clarity of purpose came in a time of haziness, heavily drugged as he recovered from surgery after a second bout with cancer, at 54. "When you're in that situation, you're mind does strange things," he recalls of watching the Pulitzer Prizes being awarded on television. "I just had this epiphany that, wow, these Pulitzers are for art and literature. There are Nobel prizes for science and economics. But there is no recognition system for people who selflessly devote their lives to children."

Leibowitz remembered one of the big lessons he had learned at P&G: Look for the "white space" in the market. "And, of course, this appeared to be a really, really big white space that was missing a player." He began working on a business plan. It took two-and-a-half years and $250,000 of his own money, but the resulting World of

Children organization would go on to become recognized as the gold standard in championing of child advocacy. "I didn't want it to be kind of a second-class, just thrown-together program," Leibowitz says. "I wanted it to be top of the line. I wanted it to be as P&G always wants you to be—No. 1 in your field. You know, if it's detergent, you want to be No. 1. If it's deodorant, you want to be No. 1. You don't want to be No. 3 or No. 4."

Leibowitz didn't just draw from his P&G years in learning to look for the space that has yet to be filled. One particular early morning encounter while at the company also drilled into him the conviction that everyone can make a difference, regardless of the scale of their positions and possessions. Just a few months on the job, as Assistant on Comet cleanser, he was approached by Stu Warshauer, who asked for Leibowtiz's help in raising money to build a residential home for the mentally challenged. Such a project wasn't new to Leibowitz, having been involved in philanthropic work "pretty much all my life." Giving was simply part of life, even growing up with immigrant parents in Brooklyn, New York, where ten families shared one bathroom. "I was probably the only kid you ever met who loved going to school because I could get to the bathroom when I got there," he recalls. "But one of things that we always had in our house was this little tin blue box and, as poor as we were, every night before we went to sleep, my grandmother insisted that each of us put a penny in that box for charity.

"There were times during World War II that we had nothing to eat but chicken fat, yet we put a penny every night in that box...It was a ritual. That was the beginning of my understanding of philanthropy, and so all through university and so on, I was always involved in charities, but they tended to be relatively small, local things, a community fund raiser or whatever." With that history in mind, Leibowitz sat down and responded to his senior's invitation to help by dashing off a letter to P&G CEO Neil McElroy in the company's internal mail, asking if he would donate something to a forthcoming dinner auction.

"What did I know?" Leibowitz says now. "I was a young kid out of school." A day or so later, at his desk early in the morning, he got a call from McElroy's office. "I almost went into shock," he says. "I was quite frightened. But he invited me up to his office, and I came up there and he was very warm and delightful. He asked me what I was doing and how long I had been at the company, and I told him. I sat down, he offered me a cup of coffee, and the next thing I knew, he gave me one of his presidential medals from when he was at the White House working for President Dwight Eisenhower and said that we could auction for this event. It raised something like $1,500, which in those days was a lot of money." The experience was transforming. "It really was a tremendous learning experience for me—one I've never forgotten. I realized that you are never too big and never too small to give back, and that giving back is not just about your local little, small group of people that may circle around you. I really learned those two things at P&G. No question about that."

Although giving was not a new concept to him, "the epiphany at Procter & Gamble was that even the big guys, the Neil McElroys of the world, have a sense that goes beyond what you and I could imagine. He had been in the White House, he was CEO for P&G—you could think that he was unapproachable, and what he proved to me was that that was not the case. "One of the other things I learned from that is never to be afraid to ask anybody if you're doing charity. I don't care who they are. Never be afraid to ask, because the worst they can do is say no. Don't be shy; you're not asking for yourself. If you're asking people to help, don't be afraid. Today, I walk into the offices of people who are billionaires; I don't flinch. I'm happy to ask them. The worst they can do is say no."

Another formative experience while at P&G was when he was part of the team working to reposition Camay. The idea was to play up the soap's super-lathering qualities, but the concept just didn't seem to be coming together with any sparkle. Leibowitz was in a meeting in Chicago with the Leo Burnett Company, when the agency's famed namesake founder came in. "Of course, all of his people stood up and they started presenting," Leibowitz remembers. "Leo sat and listened quietly and finally, when they were finished, they looked at him and he said, 'So what's the big idea?' and his people got a little bit rattled, and so they started dancing about. Well, they went on with what they were presenting and they stopped again feeling quite proud and again, Leo said, 'So what's the big idea?' This happened three times and by the end, the people were really rattled. Finally, one of the junior people stood up and said, 'Well, this will make a woman feel more sensuous." And Leo Burnett stood up and said, 'That's a big idea,' and he walked out of the room. The lesson for me was that you have got to focus, and you can't be everything to everybody. You have to be one thing, and you have to be the best at that one thing, and you have to be sure you can support that one thing." The point went deep. When Leibowitz left P&G to later run his own successful marketing consultancy, he took Burnett's lesson as "kind of a subhead of what my business stood for and it was decision by design, not by default."

"You have got to be focused, and you've got to make your decisions clear, concise, and meaningful. And, by the way, it's what I did with World of Children when I set it up."

Leibowitz's fundraising interaction with McElroy was not the only time he learned while at P&G that conventions can be circumvented sometimes. Following time as a Brand Assistant, he was sent to New Jersey to get some sales experience. It was 1967, the summer of the race riots. "It was not the best experience of my life, because you know, here I was driving around in Newark and the outlying areas, large portions of which were on fire every day, in a car that had no air conditioning, and I had to make my quotas." He quickly recognized that it was not a good idea to be on the streets much after 11 a.m. But he also realized that most supermarkets had their back doors open most of the night because they were getting deliveries. "So I started getting up at 2 a.m. and going out and making my calls starting at 3 a.m. or 4 a.m., so that by 10 a.m. or 11 a.m. I could be off the streets.

God knows, they might block the street, turn my car over; I mean, I could be dead."

He didn't tell anyone at head office what he was doing, "but I was meeting my quotas, I was getting my numbers done, I was getting the displays up. I was just doing it at 4 a.m. and 5 a.m. In hindsight, what I learned from that was that you don't always have to follow the rules exactly as they are—as long as you don't break rules and as long as you are successful." Leibowitz says, "Wisdom and knowledge are two characteristics that can live separately, but only when they live together do you have success. There are a lot of smart people out there who aren't all that successful and a lot of wise people who wind up getting killed at a very young age." Then there are those who show extraordinary character at a very young age. Leibowitz tells of Ryan Hreljac, a World of Children honoree. As an eight-year-old Catholic school student, he decided he wanted to respond to a teacher's challenge to donate $70 to give kids in Africa water. Money was tight at home, but his parents wanted to encourage him, so they said he could work for the money. He raised the $70, took it in to school, and said he wanted to build a well in Africa. "The nun looked at him and said, 'Well, Ryan, for $70 we can buy some water, but it takes $2,000 to build a well.' So Ryan went home a little depressed and sat down with his calculator and figured out that he would be 82 years old at this rate by the time he could build a well. So he decided he was going to do something else. And so he got all his friends together and they raised $2,000 to build a well."

World of Children recognized the youngster with one of its awards when he was 12—by which time he had built 36 wells in Africa and founded Ryan's Wells. Now, attending a university, he has built more than 600 wells and been named UNICEF's fresh water ambassador to the world. "If an 8-year-old child can have that kind of an impact, anybody can and should make a difference," says Leibowitz—whose own efforts were recognized by veterans of the company he credits in helping inspire him, with the Procter & Gamble Alumni Humanitarian Award of 2007.

"The truth of the matter is we are the most fortunate people on earth, and it doesn't take millions to make a difference," Leibowitz says. "You don't have to be Bill Gates to make a difference. Bill Gates does wonderful things. He is an amazing human being. But not everybody can be Bill Gates, and it's very easy to get into vapor lock and to say the problems are so big, what is my $5 going to do? What is my $10, what is my three hours a week of volunteer work going to do?" The answer: "A lot. Everything makes a difference, and everybody can and should. We have been blessed in this country with the most incredible opportunities with the most incredible lifestyle. Somebody like myself, who didn't even have a bathroom until I was 11 years old: Look at what I'm doing now. That's what so great about this country, but we can't afford to just walk away."

35

Carole Black

Social responsibility is a core value of Carole Black. Her lifetime application of the value and her steady influence have made a global impact that will outlive her. As a board member and leading advocate for V-Day—the worldwide activist group combating violence against women and girls, just one of several charitable concerns with which she is involved—Black draws on the experiences of a varied career to help make the world a better place. Although she earned recognition for her leadership at Disney and the Lifetime Network, Black traces the principles on which she operates back to her first job on graduating from college, with Procter & Gamble (P&G).

Black hails from the company's Cincinnati home ground, having graduated from Ohio State University with a degree in English literature and no real plans for business. But she was familiar with P&G and fascinated by branding, landing a Brand Assistant's position for personal care products. She was with the company for only a couple of years, "but it was a wonderful experience," she says. "The training there I think has lasted for my whole life and has served me through my entire career and even today in my philanthropic work."

Black says that her whole working life has been built on a philosophy she saw modeled at P&G: people, product, profit. "First comes the people. If you hire the very best people and you support them to be their best, you're going to get the best products, and out of that you're going to make the most profit. I have seen a lot of companies try to flip it and essentially try to figure out how they could make the most profit and work backward, and that doesn't really work. It's a longer process to start by hand-selecting the best people and supporting them the best way possible, but it's a longer-lasting way to do business."

Although she was one of only a handful of women working in brand management at P&G in the mid-60s, Black found that the company was ahead of the cultural curve in one important way—which would shape her future successes. With P&G's emphasis on knowing and serving the consumer, there was "a deep understanding of women" who shape so many buying decisions, she recalls. "That was very important with P&G—really wanting to understand and connect with the consumer—and it's one of the key principles I've always looked at in leading. It's very, very important to understand who your end user is and what that person wants, needs, and desires, and having a connection with them, heart and head." P&G did research "better than anyone else in understanding the consumer," Black says. "It was a tremendous background to understand what women were thinking and feeling and what would make a difference in their lives, and that has served me extremely well—and, of course, women and families. With all the work I've done, that was a core part of it."

Taking a break from full-time work to raise her son, Black was reminded of the quiet influence women have in the marketplace when she returned to business, working on the Sears account for an ad agency. She discovered "it was all about women; even the men's clothing was about women buying it for them. Women, I came to realize, either actually purchased or influenced about 90% of all the purchases that were going on, and that was fascinating to me, because they were not necessarily in positions of power, and yet they were in positions of huge influence. It's true today, where only 17% of Congress are females, though females are 51% of the population. But what I could see through all of this research was that if I could reach women with how good various products were and so forth, then that influenced the entire business I was involved in."

Black took that insight first to Disney, where she was instrumental in seeing video sales explode—largely by targeting women. "I was very aware that there was a lot of nesting going on at home," she says, mothers wanting to share childhood experiences associated with Disney productions with their own youngsters. Her team changed the marketing, away from children, toward moms. Within a short time, the division had become one of Disney's highest profit centers. "We started getting a lot of letters from women who had gone back to the workplace, talking about how they wanted their children to have the same experience they'd had," watching the same movies.

Black's success at Disney led to her being recruited as the first female head of an NBC station in Los Angeles. Leaning on her P&G training, "always look at the research and understand it," she determined that the way to grow an audience was to attract more women. "What were women interested in? They were interested in the community and good things that were going on, things about children and so forth. So instead of just having hard news—going against what a lot of people in the news division wanted to do—we started putting in softer stories, you might call them, but we gradually became No. 1 in every newscast."

That achievement in turn took Black to Lifetime TV, where she would enjoy the kind of success that saw her listed as one of the 100 most influential women of the century. By the time she stepped down as President and CEO in 2005, Black had built the network into a broadcasting powerhouse not only focused on women but changing their lives. Her Lifetime tenure was "an opportunity to have a strong national and even international influence on issues that were important to women," she reflects, "giving women a voice and letting them know that you're hearing them can change so much for the better. We got various laws changed and so forth, but I think we also told some really wonderful stories and it really made a difference in the lives of women and children."

Black's involvement in issues affecting women and girls continues through her philanthropic work with groups like V-Day, with which she became involved through her Lifetime connection with Eve Ensler, creator of the groundbreaking play, *The Vagina Monologues*. "Empowering women has such an incredible positive effect on the world," Black says as she considers how her early P&G days first oriented her to the often quietly pivotal role woman play and then equipped her to serve and advocate for them. "I've watched young girls who had been very damaged that now, 10 years later, are young leaders in various countries. It's been extraordinary to see difference that can be made by just understanding them and assisting them not just to survive, but to actually prevail and be in leadership roles. What a difference it came make; just a little bit of help can go a long way."

From her years of branding and storytelling, Black knows that inspiration can often be shared best through an individual, so she tells of Ensler's encounter with Agnes, a Masai from the Rift Valley in Kenya. The pair met when Ensler was visiting Africa. Ensler had heard of Agnes' efforts to save others from the genital mutilation she had experienced as a child. She would walk from village to village with a small anatomical model to explain why the traditional cutting was so harmful. By the time Ensler met her, Agnes' foot-weary efforts had seen 1,500 girls spared a similar fate. Ensler asked Agnes what her organization could do to help, Black recounts. "And she said, 'Well, you could buy me a jeep so I can go more places.' So we bought her a jeep and a few years later, she'd saved 4,500 girls." When Ensler then asked what V-Day could do more to help, Agnes told how she wanted to build a safe house for girls. "She's now built two houses with the help of V-Day, all run locally," Black reports. "She had so changed what was going on...she went from having her life threatened to being elected deputy mayor of the town that she was in. Just recently, she decided to run for parliament and she is revered now in Kenya. So the world changed through this one woman who made a decision that what happened to her wouldn't happen to other girls.

It's just a cultural thing that can be changed. I've seen the power of what one person can do. And I've seen it in so many countries around the world; it really is extraordinary."

Ironically, part of Black's motivation for working to see other women get equal opportunities is that she was not denied them. The first female study body president at her high school, she was "always was able to work with people or be with people where they didn't care if I were a male, a female, or kumquat, as long as I could do the work. I just found that I got tremendous support in leadership roles from men and from women and so I was obviously an advocate for other women having that opportunity too," Black says. "My whole life, I have felt very fortunate to have been supported in being in leadership roles and realizing that it didn't matter whether someone was male or female, they could still lead."

For those starting up the leadership ladder, Black counsels: "When you are in a position of power, use that power to do good. It's very important to give back—not just for the world but for yourself. There's no greater way to grow and to feel deep satisfaction then to give back to the world." Additionally, she urges, "be there for people you are working with when they need help. Because everyone needs some guidance, and everyone needs a helping hand. You get to where you are not by yourself; all of us are interdependent." Perhaps with her former Disney world in mind, she adds that "it's a very small world… just remember that everything that you have, you have because other people were there for you, and then give back in that same way."

36

Dian Alyan

Inspired by personal grief to help others in need, Dian Alyan credits her Procter & Gamble (P&G) career with providing the backbone and discipline that has turned heartbreak into action that is changing lives around the world. Knowing how to sell shampoo has helped her provide shelter for children in more than half a dozen countries, an ongoing mission that earned her the P&G Alumni Network's Humanitarian Award in 2009. The flame of her efforts was lit five years previously by the tsunami that devastated her Indonesian homeland. The U.S.-based professional lost 40 members of her extended family in the natural disaster that swept through Asia. Despite having a newborn son, Alyan felt she had to respond. "It would have been easier to send a one-time donation and go on with life," she says. "But I felt really compelled. That's my area, and those are my people. If I don't do anything, who will?"

Instead of just offering a one-time donation to relief efforts, Alyan founded the GiveLight Foundation to help children orphaned by wars and natural disasters. And in the years since, as it has grown, she has drawn on her P&G experience to lead and shape the volunteer effort.

Having graduated as an engineer, Alyan joined the company in Jakarta with a view to earning some wider business experience before moving on to other ventures, but she soon found the values she encountered echoed those of her upbringing.

Raised in a small town on the island of Sumatra, in Aceh province, Alyan was encouraged to strive for excellence by parents, and a dad in particular, for whom "A was not enough. He would ask me, 'Where's the plus in the A?'" Alyan found a similar environment at P&G, where she started work as part of the Vick's Throat Drops team. She quickly discovered that "being good is not good enough, that you have to constantly try to be better and to be best...When consumers are already happy, you're not." That pursuit of excellence "really resonated with me," she recalls. "The desire to live your best life and to be your best—I was able to channel that in P&G."

Alyan also appreciated learning about leadership. "At P&G, especially in brand management, you really have to know how to lead, because you're not working just in your own discipline. You have to lead multidisciplinary areas. I think I learned the art of management and the art of getting things done through the work of other people." Before transferring to P&G operations in America, Alyan gained formative experience through her involvement in the launch of shampoo leader Pantene in the Indonesian market—a success that caught the attention of U.S. leaders. The first major lesson, she says, was the importance of lining up one's team correctly. Some colleagues in the Indonesian launch group had reservations about the project. "I learned that you need first to convince your own team, and then you convince the management; this is how we will define success from a volume and profit perspective—and then you translate that into the local market," Alyan says. "The bigger challenge, though, is how to define what the staff looks like, and then you drive yourself and your own team to achieve that."

With a goal in mind, then there is the question of the right strategy. Alyan recognized that, for Pantene, the Western path would not work. "Take, for example, the advertisement," she says. "All the beautiful shots that we get in the U.S., they're all women with blonde hair." But blonde hair is not something people in Indonesia aspire to have, "so even from a positioning perspective, you need to know what the local consumer wants." Alyan applied these insights to GiveLight. She decided early on that the focus would not just be on Indonesia.

She wanted a bigger, global vision—and as a result, the charity has expanded from caring for 50 orphans in Aceh to more than 800 in eight countries.

Alyan also knew that although philanthropy may be different to business, those involved still need a sense of fulfillment. Commercial investors who are donors "need to know what is in it for them." While GiveLight is run by volunteers, Alyan applies the same kind of rigorous standards that would be found in the business world. With as many as 50 people at any one time seeking a volunteer position with her organization, Alyan tells prospective team members, "It's tough to get in, but once you get in, it's tough to get out." She interviews candidates and conducts performance reviews every six months to a year. "I let go of volunteers if they don't perform," she admits.

"The message is that if you want to work here, although it's volunteering per se, it is not something you can take lightly. If you have a skill set and you want to work hard, okay, but you need to perform in order to be able to stay and contribute, because a lot of people are interested." It may sound tough, "but if you have a principle, people actually value that," she has found. Alyan's no-nonsense approach extends to meetings. Nursing a baby in the early days of the charity, she was frustrated when others would turn up late for appointments. "So I started a new principle: If you come late, you pay a dollar for every minute that you're late. Every single meeting we collect at least $30 to $60—and that's enough to feed a child somewhere in a Third World country for an entire month."

At the same time, Alyan sees a difference between taking control of a meeting and micromanaging every decision that is made there. "Once you define what success looks like, you need to empower people, and you need to trust people to figure out the best way to deliver results," she says. "In general, when people come to work, they want to be their best, they want to deliver the best results, and when they feel empowered and they can see what success looks like and they share that with you, then I truly believe that people will perform at their very best. "That's what I have seen in my own team. We define the success upfront, talk a little bit about the strategy, and they execute. You see results immediately, and when people see results, they become more excited, and they want to do more." There also needs to be "a compelling mission" for people to align themselves, and that is strongly identified in caring for widows and orphans. "Most of us have a soft spot for them." When that is coupled with "people who tend to want to excel in what they do," the results can be dramatic.

Alyan was reminded of this at a recent fundraiser attended by 800 people. "I felt like there are so many people in the world who have good hearts, but they just don't know where to start. We can show them changed lives from their work. One example is Nursamawi, a young orphan girl that GiveLight has supported for an extended period. Five years on, she is in college with a scholarship, a 3.7 GPA, and dreams of pursuing her Master's degree in Europe. These kinds of stories really, really excite me, and I feel like there are so many orphans out there who are just like that," says Alyan. "They are probably as smart as some of our own children, but they don't have the resources. So, what I'm doing is just basically filling that gap and giving people here, my friends who are endowed with the sources, the opportunity to really shape lives and change destinies of people whom they have never met. I approach this as a business and certainly not as a hobby. After the tsunami, I worked around the clock for a whole year while being a new mother myself. My youngest was six months old. I was nursing, and I remember I only stopped to nurse him. I only stopped to feed myself and to do my prayers, and other than that, I was working 24/7 for the entire year and I loved every minute of it."

Fueled by both her personal loss and her faith, Alyan feels that P&G helped shape and prepare her for her current role. "I feel so blessed that through GiveLight, I have become the person I always wanted to be. I was able to accomplish a lot because of my husband, whose role was critical from day one as my number-one supporter of the project. He dedicated his life to the cause by caring for our young boys when I ran meetings and did hundreds of presentations. He also traveled with me to our orphanage and helped with crafting the design principles for our first orphanage in Aceh. I am able to utilize my skill set in a way that benefits others. At P&G we improve consumers' lives; that's one our slogans, right? But with GiveLight, I truly feel that I not only improve the lives of orphans and the poor, but am able to actually shape their future and their destiny, and it doesn't actually take much if you look from a dollar perspective. You can sponsor a child somewhere for $30, and for most of us, what is $30 a month?"

Alyan is also thankful that, through her P&G ties—she left the company in 1999—she gets many invites to speak to other businesses about GiveLight. One of them, Cisco, has become one of the charity's largest supporters, donating around $250,000 over the past five years. When Alyan speaks about GiveLight, she tells of wanting to do for orphans and the needy what Conrad Hilton did for hotels. "I mean I want to build the most beautiful homes around the world, and my clients would be the poorest of the poor, the orphans or the forgotten," she says. There is room for everyone to help make a difference, she emphasizes. Alyan tells of a Sri Lankan family that donated two acres of land worth about $50,000 to be the site of an orphanage, while someone from Germany gave $35,000 to GiveLight's project in Aceh.

Then there were the school children in the San Francisco Bay area Alyan now calls home who sold pizzas, tee-shirts, fruit, "and anything you can think of" to raise $11,000 for GiveLight. "They called me to the school; they gave me the money. I was so happy. It was in boxes full of coins and dollars; I couldn't even lift it. Somebody actually had to bring a trolley and pull it to my car. I brought that money to Indonesia, and we bought the first stones and bricks and cement to build the first home, and I will never, ever, ever, ever forget that."

Epilogue by Ed Artzt, Former CEO

I hope you enjoyed this book about the importance of core values to Procter & Gamble's (P&G's) success. It is the only book about P&G that examines the way P&G's employee alumni experienced their own personal transformation from trainees to successful managers. In each case, the resulting bond inspired by P&G's unique culture has led to a lifetime of values to live and work by, in addition to lasting friendships with colleagues. The underlying theme that emerges is clearly that P&G is all about people and values, and it always has been. P&G's values go back to the principles of "just and right dealings" upon which William Procter and James Gamble built the company in 1837, one hundred seventy-four years ago. Each successive generation of leadership has enunciated them over and over, and now our alumni have eloquently expressed them in their own words and in terms of their own life experience.

Saatchi & Saatchi's Ken Roberts describes P&G's most defining value as "purpose—to improve the lives of the people of the world." Boeing's Jim McNerney recalls, "The difference between right and wrong is the same in a business as it is at home, and that was easily understood at P&G." In my own words to P&G employees at our 1993 year-end meeting, I said, "I am proud to work for a company that wants to be the best at everything it does and embraces the high standards necessary to achieve high goals. We all work for a winner. I value working for a company that places integrity above all else—a company that believes in always trying to do the right thing; always obeys the law—even when competitors might not; always practices fair dealing with partners, customers, suppliers, and agents. I am proud to work for a company that operates by principle and is willing to forgo expedient compromise to preserve its principles, even under criticism, coercion, or political pressure."

Virtually every alumni interviewed for this book gave tribute to P&G's core value of commitment to the development of its people. North America Pharmaceutical's Kay Napier said, "It's indoctrination like nothing you can experience anywhere else. You live in an environment of excellence, with smart people. You aspire to do everything to the Nth degree, the right way." Walmart's Jane Thompson called it the "Ecosystem Culture, built on trust, checks and balance, and innovation, where people are expected to lead thinking and initiatives early in their careers."

Former P&G Chairman Neil McElroy would have loved this book. Some fifty-seven years ago (my first year with P&G), he told us, "The people of a business are motivated to their highest level of performance only if they are given plenty of individual responsibility and if superior performance is suitably recognized." I have never forgotten his words, and I have quoted him often. McElroy epitomized P&G's attitude toward its people. I remember an incident during my first days in Cincinnati. I was in awe when I arrived. I remember one morning riding up the crowded elevator with McElroy, his worn leather briefcase bursting with his overnight mail. He had a big smile and a booming voice, and he warmly greeted everyone in the elevator, addressing those he knew by their first name.

I recall that almost all the people I worked with were like that— genuine, respectful, and caring. I bonded quickly in that work environment. I would also add that I am immensely proud to have worked for a company that places character above all other qualities in the people it hires, and then invests tirelessly in their training, development, and progress throughout their careers. No wonder the company has produced so many successful leaders. No wonder, too, that P&G has been able to successfully grow its business outside the United

States mostly organically over the years. The key: Young P&G hires in each country, led initially by experienced imported P&G managers, who knew from their own training how to quickly develop young people to handle important responsibility. I would certainly urge others in positions of responsibility to embrace the core values for their institutions that would define their paths to lasting success.

Appendix

Core values are indeed strategic. The conclusions from the many voices featured in this book are not merely subjective views. They are echoed in the quantitative research findings that are gleaned from the input of more than 1,000 Procter & Gamble (P&G) alumni from around the globe. This research was designed and analyzed by Robert Petrausch, Ed.D, Columbia University, Associate Professor of Mass Communication at Iona College and a 25-year veteran of corporate communication roles within leading companies. Dr. Petrausch and his colleagues at Columbia, including Victoria Marsick, Ph.D., Professor of Education and Codirector of the J.M. Huber Institute for Learning in Organizations at Columbia University, have been pivotal to understanding Transformational Leadership. We are grateful for their interest and contributions to this book.

Dr. Petrausch's research team clearly substantiated the important role of specific core values and principles learned from the responses of nearly 1,000 former employees of P&G. He concluded that these core values were significant and formidable to building leadership traits as witnessed by the individuals featured in this book. Most importantly, these core values are a part of thousands of P&G employees today and have materially affected tens of thousands of others, their families, communities, and Fortune 500 companies currently led by P&G alumni.

The highlights of the key learning from the research are summarized in the sections that follow. The details of the research questions and responses follow the write-up.

I. P&G Alumni Quantitative Research Details and Summary of Key Learning

What do nearly 1,000 alumni from around the world believe about the value of the P&G experience? The web survey indicates a strong bond between the P&G organization and its alumni. Alumni from all over the world volunteered to participated in the survey and to provide their answers to questions about several aspects of their P&G experiences...the company's core values; the learning, training, and development they received; the quality of leadership they observed; the loyalty they feel to the company; the company's recruiting system; the company's influence in business and communities; and the level of connectivity with members and chapters. Members were told that data would be used for an upcoming book project and that their contribution would be valuable to the P&G Alumni Network leaders and members.

The respondents showed a sense of commitment and loyalty to their old company by readily sharing their opinions on how the training and learning they received at P&G has influenced their life and career. These talented people have largely moved on to successful careers at other organizations, and some have climbed to the pinnacle of success at many of America's leading companies.

The survey data points to several aspects of Transformational learning and leadership existing at P&G. The stories provided by notable alumni can be compared to the survey data to form a more complete picture of what aspects of P&G experiences of alumni shape their own lives and the degree of success and accomplishment they achieve later in life.

What is perhaps the most notable and interesting about the information gleaned from the survey data is that the "experience" the alumni had while at P&G may well be the most significant of their careers. As such, it may also be the cornerstone of how other companies can create high-performance organizations and teams in the twenty-first century. P&G is not a perfect organization, but it appears that one of its key strengths is its willingness to learn about itself from the alumni who care about its future.

Major Themes Drawn from Survey of P&G Alumni

1. Values

Values are shown to be central to the success of P&G and its alumni. They play an important role in the development of the successful leaders and high-achieving performers who once worked at this legendary company. In the web survey, the highest-scoring value among P&G alumni was for "Doing the Right Thing" (77%). This value appears to be at the heart of the P&G culture, and it resonates with alumni at all levels of the organization. Other high-scoring values include "Respect for the Contribution of Others" (66%); "Merit Determined by Performance" (57%); "Sharing Credit for Success" (53%); "Honest Evaluation of Causes of Poor Performance" (53%); and "Concern for the Well-Being of Partners, Customers, and Community" (49%).

When asked which values P&G alumni sought to incorporate in their work or community service role after leaving P&G, "Doing the Right Thing" (86%) once again scored the highest. This clearly indicates that P&G alumni were consistent in picking the value they admired the most when at the company and in their work and lives after leaving P&G. "Sharing Credit for Success" (73%) and "Respect for Contribution of Others" (78%) also scored high among the values that P&G alumni incorporate into their work life after their service at P&G.

Since leaving the company, many P&G alumni cannot determine whether or not the founding values of P&G are being sustained or lost with new generations of employees. However, a little over one-third of the alumni who participated in the web survey believe that the founding values of P&G are being fostered and sustained. Many P&G alumni maintain contact with the organization through membership in and activities of the P&G Alumni Network, the organization's website, the newsletter, and sponsored events throughout the country and around the globe.

2. Transfer of Knowledge (Learning)

Management training is often imposed on people in organizations, and they tend to dislike it and even question its importance. However, at P&G, management training is part of the manager's development process, is valued as a significant part of their learning experience, and is considered important at the time of promotion. Furthermore, although many companies by their own admission have failed to develop excellent managers, P&G has accomplished the opposite. It has produced an inordinate number of managers who have gone on to lead some of America's leading companies. Steve Ballmer at Microsoft, Jeff Immelt at GE, Jim McNerney at Boeing, Scott Cook at Intuit (Quicken/QuickBooks/TurboTax), and Meg Whitman (formerly at eBay) are only a few who have moved into the position of CEO in leading companies.

When asked in the P&G web survey how P&G alumni transfer their learning and leadership skills to other organizations, a decisive majority (78%) said they modeled their leadership approaches after their P&G bosses. This is a significant finding because one study, by the Hay Group in 1989, reported that fewer than 25% of employees in this country believe they are well managed. That number may be even smaller today, given the economic turmoil of the U.S. economy.

In addition, a large number of P&G alumni (60%) said they incorporate key elements of their P&G training into existing training and development programs at other companies—a testament to the value they placed on their P&G training. An even more important statistic is that 50% of the surveyed P&G alumni said that they base many of their own leadership styles on the key values they learned at the company.

An overwhelming majority of survey responders (85%) said they believed that P&G is a learning organization, one that learns continuously and transforms itself. Learning takes place in individuals, in teams, in the organization as a whole, and even in the communities with which the organization interacts. This finding shows overwhelming support from alumni in how P&G succeeds in making the transfer of knowledge work for its employees and managers.

An unprecedented number of P&G alumni (95%) believe that P&G views the process of learning and other means of professional development as the best means of improving performance. This finding illustrates how respect for learning has penetrated the P&G organization and is highly valued by the alumni, even after they have left the company. Only a small minority (5%) of respondents said "No, not really" when asked if they believed P&G was a learning organization.

Although this view of learning as practiced at P&G might seem unrealistic to many outside observers who have never worked at the company, an unmistakable majority (75%) of the P&G alumni reported that P&G invests in learning, both individually and corporate-wide, with ongoing consistency. Only a tiny fraction (4%) of alumni responded that P&G does not invest in learning at all. Finally, the alumni believe that the consistent focus on and investment in learning at P&G is much more pervasive than at other organizations they have worked after leaving P&G.

3. *Learning Influences*

At P&G, learning is derived from four approaches:

1. Formal training
2. Learning by doing
3. Cultural or environmental influences
4. Role model and mentoring

P&G emphasizes learning within the organization and invests substantial resources and money to ascertain that learning truly benefits its employees.

A majority of P&G alumni (62%) supported the notion that "Learning by Doing" is the best way to grasp functional skills. This experiential learning approach is popular within the P&G training regimen and often accounts for the high level of success that P&G alumni achieve when they move into other companies and other industries. When it comes to building expertise in project and leadership work at P&G, alumni give high marks to "Learning by Doing." A large fraction (31%) of respondents reported that opportunities to learn by doing in early leadership roles were very important in their own development.

In addition, an important method of learning was found in the role model or mentoring experience. P&G alumni generally admire and fondly remember the mentoring, coaching, and role models that shaped their early experience at the company. Through these experiences at P&G, these young alumni learned to manage risks, take chances, and grow as managers in diverse jobs within the company. For the majority of P&G alumni (54%), oral stories passed down to employees and the role of their bosses in telling stories of their own P&G experiences accounted for the top two ways the P&G experience was transmitted from generation to generation.

At P&G, cross-functional collaboration is highly valued as a way to move up the corporate ladder and succeed in effecting change within the company. Marketers, engineers, chemists, lab staff, financial analysts, and the sales force learn to work together to develop and introduce successful and innovative products to the marketplace. A large fraction of P&G alumni (46%) reported in the web survey that cultural/environmental influences were most important in ensuring that cross-collaboration could work best within the organization.

P&G is widely recognized as having one of the best (if not the best) training and development programs in consumer branding, marketing, advertising, and public relations. But in addition, P&G alumni have become leaders in more fields than from nearly any other Fortune 500 company. Recruiters, consultants, graduate MBA directors, and journalists often support this claim when writing or being interviewed in business publications about management development programs.

When P&G alumni were asked in the web survey what is the best way for others to be taught training and development skills, and project initiation and leadership, a large fraction (45%) noted that role models or mentoring experiences were the most important. This judgment can be traced back to the training and mentoring experiences these alumni had as young P&G employees. The alumni also admire their role models at P&G because they believe these individuals set the highest standards in the industry and they provided a learning environment that was unmatched anywhere else. A very large majority (70%) of respondents said the confidence in their own skills to lead and train is what accounts for P&G's long-term commitment to learning and the success of employees in various roles after they leave the organization. But nearly half (48%) said that their internalization and commitment to the underlying core values of the company accounted for the success of alumni in various roles after they left the company.

One of the core competencies of the P&G organization is its ability to develop insights leading to innovative solutions for the marketplace. P&G is a powerhouse in the branding and innovation of new products in the marketplace. The alumni overwhelmingly believe that the twin pillars of "Cultural and Environmental Influences" (36%) and "Learning by Doing" (34%) are the key factors that account for the success in developing insights that lead to innovative solutions in the marketplace.

The alumni also believe that working in a corporate culture that values innovation and new solutions creates an environment in which employees can contribute, thrive, and succeed. In recent years, P&G has also turned to outside suppliers and individuals to help them sustain the company's reputation for innovation. They point to this new move as P&G looking for new vehicles to support the drive for innovations, by leveraging the best ideas from any possible source.

Finally, in the category of persuasion skills in "Selling Proposals and Recommended Actions," P&G alumni were divided in their web survey responses on the best way to make this happen. Large portions of the alumni supported formal training (25%), learning by doing (30%), and role model and mentoring experiences (36%). Each approach certainly has its own benefits. Formal training offers the organization a systematic approach to reach employees who need this type of training and development. Experiential learning ("Learning by Doing") is flexible and can match an individual with specific people in the organization who have mastery in specific areas. Role models/mentoring have the advantage of letting highly skilled and valued individuals in the organization provide their expertise where it is most needed...and is a training and development experience that can be delivered efficiently to all levels in an organization, over an extended period of growth and development by the individual. These responses appear to indicate that the culture of learning and improving that permeates P&G seems to include all three of these approaches in roughly comparable balance.

4. Success in Business and Elsewhere

One of the great tributes to the P&G alumni is that they are sought after by other companies, nonprofit organizations, and even governmental entities around the world. P&G's reputation has remained steady in both good and bad economic times. The company's bedrock values, its marketing and technical expertise, and HR recruiting approaches continue to be emulated around the world.

When asked what accounts for the unusually high success of P&G alumni in business and elsewhere, the responders (83% of total responders) cited three primary reasons in the web survey:

1. The mind-set of high performance expectations and a desire to continuously improve (29%). This mind-set is pervasive throughout the company and is instilled in every young recruit to the company.

2. The leadership training, mentoring, and work skills learned at P&G (28%). This makes sense because P&G has produced leaders in almost every business segment and is considered a leader in management training for both its young employees and its senior managers. Most P&G alumni can still remember their first day on the job, the mentors who helped them exceed expectations, and the work skills that accompanied them even after they left the company.

3. The recruitment process at P&G and the kind of people who are attracted to the company in the first place (26%). Many in the management field accept that it may be tougher to get into P&G than it is to get into a top Ivy League school. The company takes its time in the recruitment process, and only the best candidates are vetted and selected for employment.

   Not only were Steve Ballmer, CEO of Microsoft, and Jeff Immelt, chairman of GE, hired by P&G as young recruits to the organization, it is believed that they shared the same cubicle at some point while they worked their way up the organization.

Many companies are often so bottom line-oriented that they focus single-mindedly on making the numbers today and sacrifice long-term performance that could help them secure their future. However, a huge majority of P&G alumni (76%) agreed with the view that P&G strives for an effective balance on both short-term and long-term goals. This is an impressive number when one considers that many U.S. managers believe that concentrating on long-term performance is a luxury they no longer have in their organizations.

Another important finding from the P&G alumni web survey is that when asked to identify P&G's greatest strengths, they cited two very different factors at about equal levels: (1) the company's business success (37%) and (2) the company's values and mission (36%). Most P&G alumni seem to support the idea that if a company is to be successful in the marketplace, it cannot have financial success without also being committed to values. Moreover, just as a car cannot be driven without fuel, a company cannot succeed in the long term without providing a system of values that is accepted by employees and honored by its management.

The key question often asked by competitors and others is why P&G employees and alumni are continually sought after by recruiters and consultants. P&G alumni reported in the web survey that although the P&G brand management program, business success, and leadership training at the company matter a lot, the main reason that recruiters and consultants seek them is the consistently strong employee talent base throughout the company.

As a unique cohort, P&G alumni have made major contributions to many fields of endeavor. Since leaving P&G, most alumni members (63%) report that their most significant contributions have been in the business field. However, one-third (33%) of alumni report contributions in the fields of government, nonprofit humanitarian work, consulting, and education. In short, P&G alumni contributions can be found all over the world. These talented men and women have often challenged the way businesses and other organizations contribute to society. Furthermore, they have taken what P&G has taught them and provided new ways of thinking and taking action in many areas of the global society.

5. Development of People and Managers

P&G is a world leader in developing people within its own organization. Many people from this talent pool move on to become successful alumni members who carry their valuable training to other organizations around the world.

When asked from which individuals they learned the most about the importance of developing people at P&G, a majority of the alumni on the web survey (55%) cited their bosses. In the early 1950s, 1960s, and 1970s, these bosses were mostly men who grew up in a male-dominated work culture. They were smart, talented, and the best-of-the-best in the P&G culture. In the post-1980s, women bosses would play an increasingly greater role and participate in the management development process within P&G. The alumni at P&G came to rely on mentors (14%) for advice on how to move ahead in the organization, how to lead teams, and how to grow the business. The alumni also cited P&G management (25%) whose skills, behaviors, and values inspired them.

6. Continuous Improvement—Job Performance and Excellence

Many companies tend to give "lip service" to the concepts of excellence and continuous improvement. Companies introduce slogans, mission statements, and "flavor of the month" motivational and incentive programs as ways to improve job performance and productivity.

Fortune magazine's "Reputation Survey Issue" is a good guide for which companies take continuous improvement and excellence seriously. P&G is consistently on that list. A remarkably large majority

(74%) of P&G alumni who participated in the web survey said that when compared to other organizations where they have worked, P&G focused on continuous improvement for job performance and business results more directly than others. By comparison, only a small fraction (6%) said "no, not really" or "no, not at all" when asked if a focus on continuous improvement and excellence existed in their experience at P&G.

7. Connectivity Within the Alumni Network and Loyalty to P&G

When most people leave an organization, they move on with their lives and typically forget about their old organization. They might stay in contact with a few friends and follow the activities of their old organization in the media. However, at P&G, the alumni have a strong network, a website, and chapters and events around the world that they can attend to meet former colleagues and retain some contact with the company. The biannual global reunions, held at different locations around the work, attract between 500 and 600 alumni attendees for a weekend of shared learning and camaraderie.

Most organizations would envy the rapport and positive feelings that P&G alumni have for each other and their old company. When asked in the alumni web survey what they liked most about the P&G Alumni Network, the largest fraction (39%) noted the connections with friends and colleagues from around the world. The next largest group (28%) of alumni said that networking connections were important. Job leads, chapter events, newsletters, and the website composed the remaining items on the list that alumni liked about the company.

Finally, the persistent question on the minds of recruiters, top-tier consultants, leaders in business, and even leading academicians, is this: What accounts for the loyalty of P&G alumni to each other and to the company? The alumni themselves cited four reasons they remain loyal to the company:

1. Relationships with past friends and colleagues. The power of shared experiences probably doesn't adequately explain this. It is more likely the shared success culture that comes from the emphasis on developing people driven by the practice of hiring only at the entry level and promoting from within the company.

2. A good working experience at the company, where there is a shared value system that is lived by individuals and readily observed that the management lives the value system they advocate for the organization.

3. Good training and development of skills while at the company. Again, where the future leaders have to come from within the employee group...and there is essentially no hiring from outside the company for levels above the entry level...the commitment to the development of those in any organization by the leadership is felt strongly.

4. Shared values instilled while at the company. These core values are not only held broadly at the company, as indicated in the research and in the stories in the chapters; they continue to be part of most alumni when they leave the company.

8. Other Important Data from the Survey

The alumni responding to the survey represented a fairly balanced sampling of service years with the company, from the 18,000 alumni in the network. Just over 50% of alumni in the survey reported 5 to 19 years of service at P&G; 29% reported less than 5 years of service; 21% of alumni reported more than 20 years.

A significant number of survey respondents (82%) did not retire from P&G but went on to other jobs.

A majority (67%) of respondents came from three primary areas of the company: (1) Marketing and Brand Management; (2) Sales or Customer Business Development; (3) Manufacturing or Product

Supply. The balance (33%) came from Administrative, Research, and Staff functions of the company.

A large majority (78%) of respondents had some management role in the company. A much smaller fraction (19%) did not have a management role, and an expected small fraction (4%) was Executive Officers of P&G, or Executive Vice Presidents.

Most alumni left P&G for positive reasons, not negative ones. A tiny minority (2%) of the respondents did not like the working environment or culture at P&G. The majority of respondents left for better opportunities or different jobs and venues.

The three highest industry segments where the respondents reported working are (1) Consumer Packaged Goods (Including Food and Beverage); (2) Agencies/Consulting/Marketing and Media Services; and (3) Health Care and Beauty Care Products/Services/ Pharmaceuticals.

On a scale of 1 to 10, where 1 is poor and 10 is excellent, an overwhelming majority (87%) of respondents listed their overall experience at P&G as compared to their experience at other organizations in the ranges of 8 to 10. Only a small minority (13%) reported the experience at P&G compared to other organizations in the ranges of 1 to 7.

9. Details of the Online Survey Questionnaire and Responses

Summary of Research Questionnaire Data from Global Alumni Responses

Breakdown of the demographic information from 965 responders is provided at the end of the summary.

1. Which of these values plays an important role in the development of successful leaders and high-achieving performers while at P&G? (Check all that apply.)

1. Democracy of ideas	370	38%
2. Respect for the contributions of others	638	66%

3. Sharing credit for successes	511	53%
4. Honest evaluation of the causes of poor performance	513	53%
5. Shared commitment to individual success by managers	486	50%
6. Hire only at the entry level and promote only from within	415	43%
7. Merit determined by performance drives promotions and financial rewards	550	57%
8. Concern for the well-being of partners, customers, consumers, and communities	475	49%
9. Focus on improving the lives of consumers	480	49%
10. Doing the right thing	749	77%
11. The concerns of the company and employees are inseparable	343	35%
Other	175	18%

2. Which of these values did you seek to incorporate in your work, or community service roles, after your time at P&G? (Check all that apply.)

1. Democracy of ideas	443	46%
2. Respect for the contributions of others	752	78%
3. Sharing credit for successes	704	73%
4. Honest evaluation of the causes of poor performance	595	61%
5. Shared commitment to individual success by managers	505	52%
6. Hire only at the entry level and promote only from within	67	7%
7. Merit determined by performance drives promotions and financial rewards	555	57%
8. Concern for the well-being of partners, customers, consumers, and communities	544	56%
9. Focus on improving the lives of consumers	401	41%
10. Doing the right thing	837	86%
11. The concerns of the company and employees are inseparable	307	32%
Other	119	12%

3. How did you transfer your learning and leadership skills to other organizations or other endeavors after you left P&G? (Choose all that apply.)

1. Developed and led my own presentations on key values and principles	479	50%
2. Incorporated key elements into existing training and performance development programs	577	60%
3. Instituted new hiring and training programs	300	31%
4. Employed outside organizations to conduct training on key values and skills	130	14%

5. Modeled the leadership approach(es) I observed from boss(es) at P&G	745	78%
Other	163	17%

4. What types of learning take place at P&G that result in the broad skills in leadership, performance achievement, and concern for others that alumni commonly refer to? (Choose the best answer.)

1. Presentations to employees on corporate values	10	1%
2. Soliciting employees for community service volunteers or charitable donations	10	1%
3. Modeling of value-based behaviors by other employees and senior managers	244	25%
4. Rewarding of employees who practice value-based leadership, perform and achieve at the highest levels, or demonstrate concern for others	137	14%
5. Opportunities to learn by doing in early leadership roles	293	31%
6. Clear descriptions of expected behaviors in performance management system	122	13%
7. Demonstrated commitment to and involvement in your success by senior management	125	13%
Other	16	2%
Total	957	100%

For each type of learning below, which comes primarily from 1) formal training, 2) learning by doing, 3) cultural or environmental influences, and 4) role model and mentoring experiences?

5. Functional skills and expertise

1. Formal training	270	28%
2. Learning by doing	602	62%
3. Cultural/environmental influences	18	2%
4. Role model or mentoring experiences	74	8%
Total	964	100%

6. Project initiation and leadership

1. Formal training	102	11%
2. Learning by doing	332	35%
3. Cultural/environmental influences	99	10%
4. Role model or mentoring experiences	429	45%
Total	962	100%

7. Cross-functional collaboration

1. Formal training	32	3%
2. Learning by doing	253	26%
3. Cultural/environmental influences	439	46%
4. Role model or mentoring experiences	235	25%
Total	959	100%

8. Training and development of skills in others

1. Formal training	252	26%
2. Learning by doing	158	17%
3. Cultural/environmental influences	85	9%
4. Role model or mentoring experiences	461	48%
Total	956	100%

9. Development of insights leading to innovative solutions

1. Formal training	114	12%
2. Learning by doing	325	34%
3. Cultural/environmental influences	346	36%
4. Role model or mentoring experiences	171	18%
Total	956	100%

10. Persuasion skills in selling proposals and recommended actions

1. Formal training	245	25%
2. Learning by doing	294	30%
3. Cultural/environmental influences	80	8%
4. Role model or mentoring experiences	345	36%
Total	964	100%

11. What accounts for the long-term commitment to this learning and the success for employees in various roles, long after they leave the organization? (Check all that apply.)

1. Observed success of this learning in self/and or others	565	58%
2. Confidence in own skills to lead and train others	676	70%
3. Internalization and commitment to the underlying values of the company	463	48%
4. Buy-in to P&G culture and approach to learning and training	422	44%
Other	33	3%

12. What accounts for the unusually high success rate in business and elsewhere for P&G alumni after they leave the organization? (Choose the best answer.)

1. The kind of people who were recruited, who were attracted to the company in the first place	248	26%
2. The leadership training, mentoring, and work skills learned at P&G	270	28%
3. The values learned, instilled, and practiced at P&G	128	13%
4. The mind-set of high performance expectations and desire to continuously improve	280	29%
5. Openness and willingness to take risk	24	2%
Other	15	2%
Total	965	100%

13. Were there any specific role models at P&G whose skills, behaviors, or values inspired you?

Yes	643	76%
No	201	24%
Total	844	100%

14. Do you believe P&G is a learning organization in a traditional sense? A traditional learning organization is defined as one that learns continuously and transforms itself. Learning takes place in individuals, teams, the organization as a whole, and even the communities with which the organizations interacts.

1. Yes, for the most part	815	85%
2. No, not really	45	5%
3. Partial	97	10%
4. Total	957	100%

15. Compared to other organizations in which you worked, did you find that P&G focuses on continuously improving job performance and business results more directly?

1. Yes, for the most part	715	74%
2. Yes, but only from time to time	172	18%
3. No, not really	48	5%
4. Not at all	6	1%
Other	20	2%
Total	961	100%

16. Do you believe that P&G views learning as the best way to improve performance?

1. Yes, for the most part	456	48%
2. Partially, but other ways are valued and used in addition	449	47%
3. No, not really	41	4%
4. Not at all	2	0%
Other	10	1%
Total	958	100%

17. Did you find that P&G invests in learning, individually and corporately, on a consistent basis?

1. Yes, for the most part	713	75%
2. Yes, but only from time to time	184	19%
3. No, not really	43	4%
4. Not at all	4	0%
Other	13	1%
Total	957	100%

18. Did you find that the consistent focus and investment on learning was the same at P&G as at other organizations where you worked when you arrived?

1. Yes, for the most part	195	21%
2. Yes, but not as consistently or broadly	158	17%
3. No, not really	305	32%
4. Not at all	195	21%
Other	98	10%
Total	951	100%

19. Where did you find the principle focus of Management to be at P&G?

1. On making the numbers today and sacrificing long-term performance if necessary	92	10%
2. On working for long-term performance, even at the expense of today's numbers if necessary	113	12%
3. Striving for an effective balance on both short-term and long-term goals	732	76%
Other	26	3%
Total	963	100%

20. In your view, are the founding values of P&G being sustained or lost with new generations of employees?

1. Yes, for the most part	324	34%
2. No, not really	93	10%
3. Can't determine/don't know	438	45%
Other	108	11%
Total	963	100%

21. What did the P&G experience mean to you? (Check all that apply.)

1. Having supportive colleagues to share ideas with	435	45%
2. Being part of a top-ranked global corporation	746	77%
3. Being challenged and supported to exceed expectations	713	74%
4. Being part of a culture that walks its talk	483	50%
5. Making a difference in business and society	408	42%
Other	70	7%

22. Since leaving P&G, where have you made your most significant contribution? (Check one.)

1. In business	604	63%
2. In government	11	1%
3. In nonprofit and/or humanitarian work	133	14%
4. In consulting	132	14%
5. In education	43	4%
Other	34	4%
Total	957	100%

23. In what ways is the P&G experience mostly transmitted from generation to generation? (Check one.)

1. Oral stories passed down to employees	241	25%
2. Written stories or materials on P&G leadership	78	8%
3. Training programs	146	15%
4. In-house training	157	16%
5. My boss(es)	275	29%
Other	58	6%
Total	955	100%

24. From whom did you learn the most about the importance of developing people at P&G? (Check one.)

1. My bosse(es)	530	55%
2. Human resource department	25	3%
3. P&G management	235	25%
4. Mentors	132	14%
Other	35	4%
Total	957	100%

25. What do you consider P&G's greatest strength? (Check one.)

1. Its business success	349	37%
2. Its community service and outreach	4	0%
3. Its contributions to business and society	122	13%
4. Its alumni legacy	41	4%
5. Its values and mission	344	36%
Other	96	10%
Total	956	100%

26. What makes P&G employees and alumni sought after by recruiters and consultants? (Check all that apply.)

1. Brand management program	362	38%
2. Employee talent	706	74%
3. P&G's business success	447	47%
4. Leadership training	493	51%
Other	78	8%

27. What do you like most about the P&G Alumni Network? (Check one.)

1. Connections with friends and colleagues from around the world	367	39%
2. Job leads	21	2%
3. Alumni chapter and reunion events	66	7%
4. Website	22	2%
5. Newsletters	80	9%
6. Community	49	5%
7. Service opportunities	10	1%
8. Networking opportunities	263	28%
Other	56	6%

28. What would you like to see improved in the P&G Alumni Network? (Check all that apply.)

1. Job leads	334	37%
2. Website	116	13%
3. Newsletters	156	17%
4. Local alumni chapter events	341	38%
5. Global alumni reunion events	58	6%
6. Community outreach/fundraising	102	11%
7. Networking opportunities	460	51%
Other	67	7%

29. What do you think accounts for the loyalty of P&G alumni (to each other, to the company, etc.) after they leave the company? (Check all that apply.)

1. Relationships with past friends and colleagues	604	63%
2. Good working experience while at the company	608	63%
3. Good training and development of skills while at the company	396	41%
4. Values instilled	534	56%
Other	73	8%

30. On a scale of 1 to 10 (1 is poor and 10 is excellent), how would you rate your overall experience at P&G (values, results, learning, etc.) as compared to your experience at other organizations?

1. 1 Poor	2	0%
2. 2	5	1%
3. 3	3	0%
4. 4	7	1%
5. 5	8	1%
6. 6	23	2%
7. 7	81	8%
8. 8	271	28%
9. 9	287	30%
10. Excellent	276	29%
Total	963	100%

31. *How long did you work for P&G? (Check one.)*

1. Less than 5 years	279	29%
2. 5 to 10 years	333	35%
3. 11 to 19 years	154	16%
4. More than 20 years	199	21%
Total	965	100%

32. *Did you retire from P&G?*

1. Yes	177	18%
2. No	783	82%
Total	960	100%

33. *What was your primary functional area at P&G? (Check one.)*

1. Advertising support services (media, commercial production, promotion development, public relations	32	3%
2. Finance, accounting, and administrative services	77	8%
3. Human resources/recruiting	37	4%
4. Information systems/technology	68	7%
5. Manufacturing or product supply	169	18%
6. Marketing/brand management	291	30%
7. Market research	40	4%
8. Product/packaging development	60	6%
9. Sales or customer business development	181	19%
Total	955	100%

34. *What was your level of management when you left P&G? (Check one.)*

1. I was not a manager	180	19%
2. Functional associate manager	279	29%
3. Level group or department level manager	322	34%
4. Operating business unit level manager	105	11%
5. Multiple business unit manager	34	4%
6. Company officer or executive (VP or higher)	36	4%
Total	956	100%

35. What was the primary reason you left P&G? (Check one.)

1. Received an offer for more salary and advancement opportunities	195	20%
2. Wanted to live and work in a different area	152	16%
3. Wanted to work in a different industry	62	6%
4. Did not like the working environment or culture at P&G	21	2%
5. Did not feel I could reach my career goals at P&G	151	16%
6. Was asked to leave by the company (restructuring, reorganization, cutback, etc.)	55	6%
7. I did not leave the company/I retired from P&G	131	14%
Other	188	20%
Total	955	100%

36. What industry segment are you working in now or did you spend the most time in during your business career? (Check one.)

1. Consumer packaged goods (including food and beverage)	301	32%
2. Retailing/wholesaling	28	3%
3. Automotive/transportation/energy/utilities	24	3%
4. Banking/financial services/insurance services/investment services	46	5%
5. Computer hardware/software/printers/supplies	36	4%
6. Telecommunications services (including wireless)	25	3%
7. Agencies/consulting/marketing and media services	99	10%
8. Health care and beauty care products/services/pharmaceuticals	72	8%
9. Sciences/life sciences	12	1%
10. Industrial/manufacturing	54	6%
11. Consumer electronic products	12	1%
12. Business services	46	5%
13. Entertainment/media/travel/restaurant/hotels	23	2%
14. Government	7	1%
15. Nonprofit/professional associations	42	4%
16. Cultural/foundations	9	1%
Other	119	12%
Total	955	100%

FINANCIAL TIMES

In an increasingly competitive world, it is quality
of thinking that gives an edge—an idea that opens new
doors, a technique that solves a problem, or an insight
that simply helps make sense of it all.

We work with leading authors in the various arenas
of business and finance to bring cutting-edge thinking
and best-learning practices to a global market.

It is our goal to create world-class print publications
and electronic products that give readers
knowledge and understanding that can then be
applied, whether studying or at work.

To find out more about our business
products, you can visit us at www.ftpress.com.